Matter and Consciousness

Matter and Consciousness

A Contemporary Introduction to the Philosophy of Mind

Revised Edition

Paul M. Churchland

A Bradford Book
The MIT Press
Cambridge, Massachusetts
London, England

Fourth printing, 1992

Revised edition, new material © 1988 Massachusetts Institute of Technology

Original edition © 1984 Massachusetts Institute of Technology

Book design by Mary Mendell.

Jacket design by Irene Elios.

Printed and bound in the United States of America by Halliday Lithograph.

Library of Congress Cataloging-in-Publication Data

Churchland, Paul M., 1942–
    Matter and consciousness: a contemporary introduction to the
    philosophy of mind/Paul M. Churchland.—Rev. ed.
    "A Bradford book." p.   cm.
    Includes index.
    ISBN 0-262-03135-3.   ISBN 0-262-53074-0 (pbk.)
    1. Intellect.   2. Consciousness.   3. Cognition.   4. Artificial
    intelligence.   5. Neurology.   I. Title.
BF431.C47 1988   128′.2—dc 19   87-21899 CIP

For my father, who taught me how to fly, and my mother, who taught me how to see.

Contents

Preface to Revised Edition

I have been much gratified by the kind reception given the first edition of this small book, especially where it concerned the sections on neuroscience, cognitive science, and artificial intelligence. As it happens, these sections are the focus of most of the changes and additions in the revised edition. The motive for change is the dramatic progress that continues to be made in these disciplines and their expanding relevance to issues in the philosophy of mind. These research results bear directly on questions such as, what are the basic elements of cognitive activity? How are they implemented in real physical systems? And how is it that living creatures perform some cognitive tasks so swiftly and easily, where computers do them only badly or not at all?

A central conviction of the first edition was that issues in the philosophy of mind are not independent of the theoretical and experimental results of the natural sciences. That view has not changed. But developments in the sciences have. This new edition attempts to make some of the more striking of these results accessible and intelligible to a wider audience. Their philosophical significance, as I see it, lies in the support they tend to give to the reductive and the eliminative versions of materialism. But my opinion is only one of many alternatives. I invite you to make your own judgment.

Preface

Philosophers usually write their books for other philosophers, and express parenthetical hopes that the book will prove useful to students and lay readers as well. Such hopes are usually vain. In hopeful contrast, I have written this book primarily and explicitly for people who are not professionals in philosophy, or in artificial intelligence, or in the neurosciences. It is the imagination of the general reader, and of the student, that I am here aiming to capture. I do indeed have subsidiary hopes that this compact volume will prove useful, as a comprehensive summary and source book, to my professional colleagues and to advanced graduate students. But I did not write this book for them. I have written it for newcomers to the philosophy of mind.

This book was first conceived during a recent undergraduate course in the philosophy of mind, taught with the aid of familiar and long-standard texts. Since so much has happened in this field in the last fifteen years, those standard texts and anthologies are now badly dated. And while some good anthologies of very recent work are now available, they are too advanced and too expensive to be used easily with undergraduates. At the end of that course, I resolved to write a more suitable and accessible text, free of fossilized issues, swift with historical summary, and bristling with the new developments. This volume is the result.

It was written during the summer of 1982, mostly at our cottage retreat on Moose Lake in the Manitoba wilderness, where the unearthly loons voiced nightly amusement at my labors. And it was completed in midautumn at the Institute for Advanced Study in Princeton, whose resident flock of Canada geese gave similar commentary.

I have occasionally profited, however, from more substantial inspiration and instruction. I must thank first my friend and colleague, Larry Jordan, for taking me into his neurophysiology lab during 1981/82, for making me a part of his marathon Wednesday Experiments, and for being the agent of so much entertainment and priceless instruction. I must thank fellow philosophers Daniel Dennett and Stephen Stich for arranging my participation in a number of professional gatherings both in the United States and in England, and for all that they have taught me during our many pleasant and useful encounters. I am indebted to my friend and colleague Michael Stack, for what is now a decade of fruitful discussion concerning the mind and its place in nature. And I must thank above all my wife and professional colleague Patricia Smith Churchland, who has taught me more about the mind/brain than any philosopher living.

Finally, my thanks to Ken Warmbrod, Ned Block, Bob Richardson, Amelie Rorty, Cliff Hooker, and David Woodruff Smith for their various encouragements, and for their valuable criticisms of the initial draft. And I am forever indebted to the Institute for Advanced Study for the facilities with which to complete this work, and for the opportunity to launch several other more theoretical pursuits.

Paul M. Churchland
Princeton, NJ, 1983

Matter and Consciousness

Chapter 1

What Is This Book About?

The curiosity of Man, and the cunning of his Reason, have revealed much of what Nature held hidden. The structure of spacetime, the constitution of matter, the many forms of energy, the nature of life itself; all of these mysteries have become open books to us. To be sure, deep questions remain unanswered and revolutions await us still, but it is difficult to exaggerate the explosion in scientific understanding we humans have fashioned over the past 500 years.

Despite this general advance, a central mystery remains largely a mystery: the nature of *conscious intelligence*. That is what this book is about.

If conscious intelligence were still totally mysterious, there would be no useful book for me to write. But encouraging progress has indeed been made. The phenomena to be penetrated are now the common focus of a variety of related fields. Philosophy has been joined by psychology, artificial intelligence, neuroscience, ethology, and evolutionary theory, to name the principals. All of these sciences have made contributions to what used to be a purely philosophical debate, and all of them promise much more to come.

This book is an introduction to the main elements of the current philosophical/scientific debate—to the major issues, to the competing theories, to the most important arguments and evidence. In the last thirty years, philosophy itself has made significant progress on the nature of mind: mainly by unraveling the status of the mind's self-knowledge, but also by providing a clearer conception of the nature of the possible alternative theories of mind between which we must finally choose, and by clarifying what sorts of evidence are needed if we are to make a reasoned choice between them.

More important still, the empirical sciences mentioned have provided a steady flow of evidence relevant to the making of such a rational choice. Psychology has taught us some surprising things about the penetration and reliability of our introspective knowledge. (This is an important matter, since some theories of mind rely heavily on what self-conscious introspection is supposed to reveal.) Cognitive psychology and artificial intelligence have produced provocative models of cognition, which, when 'brought to life' within a suitably programmed computer, mimic closely some of the complex activities of goal-driven intelligence. The neurosciences have begun to unravel the vast microsystem of interconnected brain cells that, in living creatures, appears to execute those activities. Ethology has given us new insights into the continuities, and discontinuities, relating human intelligence with the intelligence of other creatures. And evolutionary theory has revealed the long and intricate selective processes from which conscious intelligence has slowly emerged. The evidence is still ambiguous, however, and a choice from among the relevant theories has not yet been made, so the reader of this book will have the pleasure and excitement of joining an intellectual adventure that is still very much in progress.

The discussion here opens with the most obvious of the questions in this area. What is the real nature of mental states and processes? In what medium do they take place, and how are they related to the physical world? With regard to the mind, these questions address what philosophers call the *ontological problem*. (In philosophical language, an 'ontological question' is just a question about what things really *exist*, and about what their essential nature is.) This problem is more widely known as the *mind-body problem*, and very probably you are already familiar with the most basic division in views here. On the one hand, there are *materialist* theories of mind, theories which claim that what we call mental states and processes are merely sophisticated states and processes of a complex physical system: the *brain*. On the other hand, there are *dualist* theories of mind, theories which claim that mental states and processes are not merely states and processes of a purely physical system, but constitute a distinct kind of phenomenon that is essentially nonphysical in nature.

Many of us bring strong convictions to an issue such as this, and many will think that the choice between these alternatives is easy or obvious, but it is wise to keep an open mind here, whatever your convictions, at least until you have explored the lay of the land. There are at least five radically different versions of dualism, for example, and a comparable number of materialist theories, all very different from one another as well. There are not *two* theories here from which we must choose, but more like *ten*! And some of them have been formulated only recently. The purpose of chapter 2 is to lay out all of these theories, one by one, and to try to evaluate the strengths and weaknesses of each.

Any decision made on the strength of chapter 2 alone will be premature, however, since there are a number of other compelling problems with which the mind-body problem is thoroughly intertwined.

One of these is the *semantical problem*. Where do our ordinary common-sense terms for mental states get their *meaning*? What would count as an adequate definition or analysis of those special concepts that we apply to ourselves and to other creatures with conscious intelligence? One suggestion—perhaps the most plausible one, initially—is that one learns the meaning of a term like "pain" or "sensation of warmth" simply by attaching the relevant term to the relevant kind of mental state, as it is experienced in one's own case. But this view leads to a number of problems, one of which may already have occurred to you at some point or other.

How can you be sure that the inner sensation, to which your friend (say) has attached the term "pain", is qualitatively the same as the inner sensation to which *you* have attached that term? Perhaps your friend's inner state is radically different from yours, despite its being hooked up to behavior, speech, and causal circumstances in the very same ways it is hooked up in you. Your friend would thus behave in all respect as you do, despite the hidden internal difference. The problem is that this skeptical worry, once raised, seems impossible to settle, because it appears entirely impossible that anyone should ever have *direct* experience of someone *else's* mental states, and nothing less than such experience would settle the issue.

If this is so, then it appears that none of us knows, or can know, what meaning the many terms for mental states have for other people, if indeed they have any meaning at all. One can know only what meaning they have for oneself. This is a very odd conclusion to reach about a major segment of our language. The purpose of language, after all, is public communication within a shared network of understanding.

A competing theory of meaning suggests a different source for the meaning of our ordinary psychological vocabulary. To learn the meaning of the term "pain", it is claimed, is to learn that pain is a state that is often caused by bodily damage, a state that in turn causes other inner states such as mild unhappiness or outright panic, a state that causes characteristic sorts of behavior such as wincing, nursing, and moaning. In short, the essential feature of pain is said to be a *network of causal relations* that connects any pain to a variety of other things, especially to publicly observable things.

Materialists of all persuasions tend to prefer this latter approach to meaning, partly because it leaves wide open the possibility that mental states are really physical states. There is no problem in supposing a purely physical state to have the appropriate kinds of *causal* connections essential to being a pain. And this approach does not land us swiftly in skepticism. On the other hand, it does seem to give short shrift to the inner, introspectible aspect of our mental states, the aspect on which the first approach to meaning was centered. Dualists, understandably, have tended to prefer that first approach to meaning, despite its apparently skeptical consequences. The introspectible or 'subjectively evident' qualities of our mental states represent for them some of the very essence of mentality, an essence that is beyond merely physical explanation.

You can appreciate already that no solution to the mind-body problem will rest easy without a simultaneous solution to the semantical problem. Chapter 3 will examine the major alternative solutions in detail, of which again there are several. One of them will require a thumbnail sketch of some of the elementary concepts in contemporary philosophy of science, so you may look forward to some novel and unexpected theoretical suggestions.

These issues lead naturally enough to the *epistemological problem*. (Epistemology is the study of what knowledge is, and where it comes from.) This problem has two parts to it, both very perplexing. The first arises swiftly from a worry already discussed: On what grounds has one the right to assume that other humans, for example, enjoy any mental states *at all*? Granted, the assumption that they do is one of the deepest assumptions one makes. But what exactly are the rational grounds for that assumption? To justify that assumption, what one needs to know is that the behavior of others is causally connected, in the same ways, to inner states of the same kind as those to which one's own behavior is connected. One needs to know, for example, that what is caused by a hammer blow and what causes in turn a loud "ouch!" is the *same* in others as in oneself. But that would seem again to require the impossible: the direct subjective experience of someone else's mental states.

This is called the *problem of other minds*, and it is not merely a skeptical conundrum about our fellow humans. The problem begins to look less frivolous or academic when one starts to ask seriously after the mental life of animals like the great apes, or domestic dogs, or dolphins. Do they have genuine consciousness? And the current explosion in computer technology promises a new location for the problem. How can we distinguish a truly conscious intelligence from a complex physical system built to resemble a thinking being in all of its behavior, verbal and emotional behavior included? Would there *be* a difference? How could we tell?

In sharp contrast to the opacity of the mental life of people other than oneself is the transparency of one's own mental life. Each of us is *self*-conscious. What is the nature of that curious access you have to the contents of your own mind, but to no other? How is it you are able to tell, without looking at your behavior, what you feel, think, and desire? We take it for granted, this capacity for *introspection*, but it is a most extraordinary and enigmatic talent to have. A great deal has been claimed for it by various thinkers: infallibility, by some; the feature that distinguishes mind from matter, by others. And it does present a daunting challenge to any materialist who aspires to explain it. Here some findings in psychology will prove relevant. What a successful account of introspection requires, and whether a materialist approach can ever provide such an account, will be addressed in chapter 4.

As I hope it will be clear by the time you have half of this book behind you, the nature of mind is not a purely philosophical question, but a deeply scientific question as well. To say this is not to beg any questions as to which of the alternative theories will be vindicated. But I do mean to assert that empirical research will weigh heavily, or even decisively, in determining the outcome. Which raises the question: What is the proper approach or methodology to pursue in constructing a 'science of the mind'? Here again there are differences. Should a science of conscious intelligence actively seek continuity with the network of established natural sciences (physics, chemistry, biology, and so on)? Or should it claim a discontinuous autonomy on grounds of some unique feature? (Even some materialists—the functionalists—have answered yes to this latter question.) What sorts of data should it admit as legitimate? Introspection? Behavior? Neurophysiology? These issues make up the *methodological problem*, and they are pointed toward the future. The shape of future theories hangs on these issues. Chapter 5 is devoted to their exploration.

An introductory text might well draw to a close after that discussion, but I have included here three additional chapters. As this book is written, the great majority of professional philosophers and scientists in this area are clustered around only two or three of the alternative possible solutions to the mind-body problem, and their tentative commitments on that score find expression in two especially active research programs concerning cognitive phenomena. The first is the recently formed field of *artificial intelligence*, or *AI* for short. To what extent (we may ask) is it possible to simulate or recreate the essential features of conscious intelligence with suitably programmed computers? A preliminary answer is, "To a very impressive extent," although AI researchers will be the first to admit that several basic problems remain stubbornly unsolved.

The second research program is the fast-growing field of the several *neurosciences*, those sciences concerned with the empirical study of the brain and nervous system. What light (we may ask) is thrown by neuro-physiology, neurochemistry, and comparative neuroanatomy on such matters as mental illness, learning, three-dimensional vision, and the mental life of dolphins? The answer is, "Considerable light," although neuroscientists will be the first to admit that they have only scratched the surface.

I have included these chapters to provide at least an instructive sampling of the research currently under way in these fields. They are certainly not adequate to introduce an aspiring computer scientist or neuroscientist to these fields. But they will provide some real understanding of how empirical research bears on the philosophical issues discussed in this text. (That is important because, as I hope to make clear, most of those philosophical issues are ultimately empirical in character. They will be decided by the comparative success and the relative progress displayed by alternative scientific research programs.) These chapters will also provide a lasting conceptual framework from which to address future developments concerning the mind. And they may whet your appetite for more empirical information. If they do only that, they will have served their purpose.

The concluding chapter is overtly speculative, as befits a concluding chapter, and opens with an attempt to estimate the distribution of conscious intelligence in the universe at large. Intelligence appears likely to be a fairly widespread phenomenon in the universe, and all advanced instances of it will inevitably face the problem of constructing a useful conception of just what intelligence *is*. That process of self-discovery, to judge from our own case, need not be an easy one. Neither will it be completed in a short period, if indeed it can ever be truly *completed*. But progress is still possible, here, as elsewhere in the human endeavor; and we must be prepared to contemplate revolutions in our conception of what *we* are, just as we have successfully navigated repeated revolutions in our conception of the universe that embeds us. The final section scouts the consequences of such a conceptual revolution for the contents of human self-consciousness.

This concludes my set of promissory notes. Let us now turn to the issues themselves.

Chapter 2

The Ontological Problem (the Mind-Body Problem)

What is the real nature of mental states and processes? In what medium do they take place, and how are they related to the physical world? Will my consciousness survive the disintegration of my physical body? Or will it disappear forever as my brain ceases to function? Is it possible that a purely physical system such as a computer could be constructed so as to enjoy real conscious intelligence? Where do minds come from? What are they?

These are some of the questions we shall confront in this chapter. Which answers we should give to them depends on which theory of mind proves to be the most reasonable theory on the evidence, to have the greatest explanatory power, predictive power, coherence, and simplicity. Let us examine the available theories, and the considerations that weigh for and against each.

1. Dualism

The dualistic approach to mind encompasses several quite different theories, but they are all agreed that the essential nature of conscious intelligence resides in something *nonphysical*, in something forever beyond the scope of sciences like physics, neurophysiology, and computer science. Dualism is not the most widely held view in the current philosophical and scientific community, but it is the most common theory of mind in the public at large, it is deeply entrenched in most of the world's popular religions, and it has been the dominant theory of mind for most of Western history. It is thus an appropriate place to begin our discussion.

Substance Dualism The distinguishing claim of this view is that each mind is a distinct nonphysical thing, an individual 'package' of nonphysical substance, a thing whose identity is independent of any physical body to which it may be temporarily 'attached'. Mental states and activities derive their special character, on this view, from their being states and activities of this unique, nonphysical substance.

This leaves us wanting to ask for more in the way of a *positive* characterization of the proposed mind-stuff. It is a frequent complaint with the substance dualist's approach that his characterization of it is so far almost entirely negative. This need not be a fatal flaw, however, since we no doubt have much to learn about the underlying nature of mind, and perhaps the deficit here can eventually be made good. On this score, the philosopher René Descartes (1596–1650) has done as much as anyone to provide a positive account of the nature of the proposed mind-stuff, and his views are worthy of examination.

Descartes theorized that reality divides into two basic kinds of substance. The first is ordinary matter, and the essential feature of this kind of substance is that it is extended in space: any instance of it has length, breadth, height, and occupies a determinate position in space. Descartes did not attempt to play down the importance of this type of matter. On the contrary, he was one of the most imaginative physicists of his time, and he was an enthusiastic advocate of what was then called "the mechanical philosophy". But there was one isolated corner of reality he thought could not be accounted for in terms of the mechanics of matter: the conscious reason of Man. This was his motive for proposing a second and radically different kind of substance, a substance that has no spatial extension or spatial position whatever, a substance whose essential feature is the activity of *thinking*. This view is known as *Cartesian dualism*.

As Descartes saw it, the real *you* is not your material body, but rather a nonspatial thinking substance, an individual unit of mind-stuff quite distinct from your material body. This nonphysical mind is in systematic causal interaction with your body. The physical state of your body's sense organs, for example, causes visual/auditory/tactile experiences in your mind. And the desires and decisions of your nonphysical mind cause your body to behave in purposeful ways. Its causal connections to your mind are what make your body yours, and not someone else's.

The main reasons offered in support of this view were straightforward enough. First, Descartes thought that he could determine, by direct introspection alone, that he was essentially a thinking substance and nothing else. And second, he could not imagine how a purely physical system could ever use *language* in a relevant way, or engage in mathematical *reasoning*, as any normal human can. Whether these are good reasons, we shall discuss presently. Let us first notice a difficulty that even Descartes regarded as a problem.

If 'mind-stuff' is so utterly different from 'matter-stuff' in its nature— different to the point that it has no mass whatever, no shape whatever, and no position anywhere in space—then how is it possible for my mind to have any causal influence on my body at all? As Descartes himself was aware (he was one of the first to formulate the law of the conservation of momentum), ordinary matter in space behaves according to rigid laws, and one cannot get bodily movement (= momentum) from nothing. How is this utterly insubstantial 'thinking substance' to have any influence on ponderous matter? How can two such different things be in any sort of causal contact? Descartes proposed a very subtle material substance—'animal spirits'—to convey the mind's influence to the body in general. But this does not provide us with a solution, since it leaves us with the same problem with which we started: how something ponderous and spatial (even 'animal spirits') can interact with something entirely nonspatial.

In any case, the basic principle of division used by Descartes is no longer as plausible as it was in his day. It is now neither useful nor accurate to characterize ordinary matter as that-which-has-extension-in-space. Electrons, for example, are bits of matter, but our best current theories describe the electron as a point-particle with no extension whatever (it even lacks a determinate spatial position). And according to Einstein's theory of gravity, an entire star can achieve this same status, if it undergoes a complete gravitational collapse. If there truly is a division between mind and body, it appears that Descartes did not put his finger on the dividing line.

Such difficulties with Cartesian dualism provide a motive for considering a less radical form of substance dualism, and that is what we find in a view I shall call *popular dualism*. This is the theory that a person is literally a 'ghost in a machine', where the machine is the human body, and the ghost is a spiritual substance, quite unlike physical matter in its internal constitution, but fully possessed of spatial properties even so. In particular, minds are commonly held to be *inside* the bodies they control: inside the head, on most views, in intimate contact with the brain.

This view need not have the difficulties of Descartes'. The mind is right there in contact with the brain, and their interaction can perhaps be understood in terms of their exchanging energy of a form that our science has not yet recognized or understood. Ordinary matter, you may recall, is just a form or manifestation of energy. (You may think of a grain of sand as a great deal of energy condensed or frozen into a small package, according to Einstein's relation, $E = mc^2$.) Perhaps mind-stuff is a well-behaved form or manifestation of energy also, but a different form of it. It is thus *possible* that a dualism of this alternative sort be consistent with familiar laws concerning the conservation of momentum and energy. This is fortunate for dualism, since those particular laws are very well established indeed.

This view will appeal to many for the further reason that it at least holds out the possibility (though it certainly does not guarantee) that the mind might survive the death of the body. It does not guarantee the mind's survival because it remains possible that the peculiar form of energy here supposed to constitute a mind can be produced and sustained only in conjunction with the highly intricate form of matter we call the brain, and must disintegrate when the brain disintegrates. So the prospects for surviving death are quite unclear even on the assumption that popular dualism is true. But even if survival were a clear consequence of the theory, there is a pitfall to be avoided here. Its promise of survival might be a reason for *wishing* dualism to be true, but it does not constitute a reason for *believing* that it *is* true. For that, we would need independent empirical evidence that minds do indeed survive the permanent death of the body. Regrettably, and despite the exploitative blatherings of the supermarket tabloids (**TOP DOCS PROVE LIFE AFTER DEATH!!!**), we possess no such evidence.

As we shall see later in this section, when we turn to evaluation, positive evidence for the existence of this novel, nonmaterial, thinking *substance* is in general on the slim side. This has moved many dualists to articulate still less extreme forms of dualism, in hopes of narrowing further the gap between theory and available evidence.

Property Dualism   The basic idea of the theories under this heading is that while there is no *substance* to be dealt with here beyond the physical brain, the brain has a special set of *properties* possessed by no other kind of physical object. It is these special properties that are nonphysical: hence the term *property dualism*. The properties in question are the ones you would expect: the property of having a pain, of having a sensation of red, of thinking that *P*, of desiring that *Q*, and so forth. These are the properties that are characteristic of conscious intelligence. They are held to be nonphysical in the sense that they cannot ever be reduced to or explained solely in terms of the concepts of the familiar physical sciences. They will require a wholly new and autonomous science— the 'science of mental phenomena'—if they are ever to be adequately understood.

From here, important differences among the positions emerge. Let us begin with what is perhaps the oldest version of property dualism: *epiphenomenalism*. This term is rather a mouthful, but its meaning is simple. The Greek prefix "epi-" means "above", and the position at issue holds that mental phenomena are not a part of the physical phenomena in the brain that ultimately determine our actions and behavior, but rather ride 'above the fray'. Mental phenomena are thus *epi*phenomena. They are held to just appear or emerge when the growing brain passes a certain level of complexity.

But there is more. The epiphenomenalist holds that while mental phenomena are caused to occur by the various activities of the brain, *they do not have any causal effects in turn*. They are entirely impotent with respect to causal effects on the physical world. They are *mere* epiphenomena. (To fix our ideas, a vague metaphor may be helpful here. Think of our conscious mental states as little sparkles of shimmering light that occur on the wrinkled surface of the brain, sparkles which are caused to occur by physical activity in the brain, but which have no causal effects on the brain in return.) This means that the universal conviction that one's actions are determined by one's desires, decisions, and volitions is false! One's actions are exhaustively determined by physical events in the brain, which events *also* cause the epiphenomena we call desires, decisions, and volitions. There is therefore a constant conjunction between volitions and actions. But according to the epiphenomenalist, it is mere illusion that the former cause the latter.

What could motivate such a strange view? In fact, it is not too difficult to understand why someone might take it seriously. Put yourself in the shoes of a neuroscientist who is concerned to trace the origins of behavior back up the motor nerves to the active cells in the motor cortex of the cerebrum, and to trace in turn their activity into inputs from other parts of the brain, and from the various sensory nerves. She finds a thoroughly physical system of awesome structure and delicacy, and much intricate activity, all of it unambiguously chemical or electrical in nature, and she finds no hint at all of any nonphysical inputs of the kind that substance dualism proposes. What is she to think? From the standpoint of her researches, human behavior is exhaustively a function of the activity of the physical brain. And this opinion is further supported by her confidence that the brain has the behavior-controlling features it does exactly because those features have been ruthlessly selected for during the brain's long evolutionary history. In sum, the seat of human behavior appears entirely physical in its constitution, in its origins, and in its internal activities.

On the other hand, our neuroscientist has the testimony of her own introspection to account for as well. She can hardly deny that she has experiences, beliefs, and desires, nor that they are connected in some way with her behavior. One bargain that can be struck here is to admit the *reality* of mental properties, as nonphysical properties, but demote them to the status of impotent epiphenomena that have nothing to do with the scientific explanation of human and animal behavior. This is the position the epiphenomenalist takes, and the reader can now perceive the rationale behind it. It is a bargain struck between the desire to respect a rigorously scientific approach to the explanation of behavior, and the desire to respect the testimony of introspection.

The epiphenomenalist's 'demotion' of mental properties—to causally impotent by-products of brain activity—has seemed too extreme for most property dualists, and a theory closer to the convictions of common sense has enjoyed somewhat greater popularity. This view, which we may call *interactionist property dualism*, differs from the previous view in only one essential respect: the interactionist asserts that mental properties do indeed have causal effects on the brain, and thereby, on behavior. The mental properties of the brain are an integrated part of the general causal fray, in systematic interaction with the brain's physical properties. One's actions, therefore, are held to be caused by one's desires and volitions after all.

As before, mental properties are here said to be *emergent* properties, properties that do not appear at all until ordinary physical matter has managed to organize itself, through the evolutionary process, into a system of sufficient complexity. Examples of properties that are emergent in this sense would be the property of being *solid*, the property of being *colored*, and the property of being *alive*. All of these require matter to be suitably organized before they can be displayed. With this much, any materialist will agree. But any property dualist makes the further claim that mental states and properties are *irreducible*, in the sense that they are not just organizational features of physical matter, as are the examples cited. They are said to be novel properties beyond prediction or explanation by physical science.

This last condition—the irreducibility of mental properties—is an important one, since this is what makes the position a dualist position. But it sits poorly with the joint claim that mental properties emerge from nothing more than the organizational achievements of physical matter. If that is how mental properties are produced, then one would expect a physical account of them to be possible. The simultaneous claim of evolutionary emergence *and* physical irreducibility is prima facie puzzling.

A property dualist is not absolutely bound to insist on both claims. He could let go the thesis of evolutionary emergence, and claim that mental properties are *fundamental* properties of reality, properties that have been here from the universe's inception, properties on a par with length, mass, electric charge, and other fundamental properties. There is even an historical precedent for a position of this kind. At the turn of this century it was still widely believed that electromagnetic phenomena (such as electric charge and magnetic attraction) were just an unusually subtle manifestation of purely *mechanical* phenomena. Some scientists thought that a reduction of electromagnetics to mechanics was more or less in the bag. They thought that radio waves, for example, would turn out to be just travelling oscillations in a very subtle but jellylike aether that fills space everywhere. But the aether turned out not to exist. So electromagnetic properties turned out to be fundamental properties in their own right, and we were forced to add electric charge to the existing list of fundamental properties (mass, length, and duration).

Perhaps mental properties enjoy a status like that of electromagnetic properties: irreducible, but not emergent. Such a view may be called *elemental-property dualism*, and it has the advantage of clarity over the previous view. Unfortunately, the parallel with electromagnetic phenomena has one very obvious failure. Unlike electromagnetic properties, which are displayed at all levels of reality from the subatomic level on up, mental properties are displayed only in large physical systems that have evolved a very complex internal organization. The case for the evolutionary emergence of mental properties through the organization of matter is extremely strong. They do not appear to be basic or elemental at all. This returns us, therefore, to the issue of their irreducibility. Why should we accept this most basic of the dualist's claims? Why be a dualist?

Arguments for Dualism   Here we shall examine some of the main considerations commonly offered in support of dualism. Criticism will be postponed for a moment so that we may appreciate the collective force of these supporting considerations.

A major source of dualistic convictions is the religious belief many of us bring to these issues. Each of the major religions is in its way a theory about the cause or purpose of the universe, and Man's place within it, and many of them are committed to the notion of an immortal soul—that is, to some form of substance dualism. Supposing that one is consistent, to consider disbelieving dualism is to consider disbelieving one's religious heritage, and some of us find that difficult to do. Call this the *argument from religion*.

A more universal consideration is the *argument from introspection*. The fact is, when you center your attention on the contents of your consciousness, you do not clearly apprehend a neural network pulsing with electrochemical activity: you apprehend a flux of thoughts, sensations, desires, and emotions. It seems that mental states and properties, as revealed in introspection, could hardly be more different from physical states and properties if they tried. The verdict of introspection, therefore, seems strongly on the side of some form of dualism—on the side of property dualism, at a minimum.

A cluster of important considerations can be collected under the *argument from irreducibility*. Here one points to a variety of mental phenomena where it seems clear that no purely physical explanation could possibly account for what is going on. Descartes has already cited our ability to use language in a way that is relevant to our changing circumstances, and he was impressed also with our faculty of Reason, particularly as it is displayed in our capacity for mathematical reasoning. These abilities, he thought, must surely be beyond the capacity of any physical system. More recently, the introspectible qualities of our sensations (sensory 'qualia'), and the meaningful content of our thoughts and beliefs, have also been cited as phenomena that will forever resist reduction to the physical. Consider, for example, seeing the color or smelling the fragrance of a rose. A physicist or chemist might know everything about the molecular structure of the rose, and of the human brain, argues the dualist, but that knowledge would not enable him to predict or anticipate the quality of these inexpressible experiences.

Finally, paraphsychological phenomena are occasionally cited in favor of dualism. Telepathy (mind reading), precognition (seeing the future), telekinesis (thought control of material objects), and clairvoyance (knowledge of distant objects) are all awkward to explain within the normal confines of psychology and physics. If these phenomena are real, they might well be reflecting the superphysical nature that the dualist ascribes to the mind. Trivially they are *mental* phenomena, and if they are also forever beyond physical explanation, then at least some mental phenomena must be irreducibly nonphysical.

Collectively, these considerations may seem compelling. But there are serious criticisms of each, and we must examine them as well. Consider first the argument from religion. There is certainly nothing wrong in principle with appealing to a more general theory that bears on the case at issue, which is what the appeal to religion amounts to. But the appeal can only be as good as the scientific credentials of the religion(s) being appealed to, and here the appeals tend to fall down rather badly. In general, attempts to decide scientific questions by appeal to religious orthodoxy have a very sorry history. That the stars are other suns, that the earth is not the center of the universe, that diseases are caused by microorganisms, that the earth is billions of years old, that life is a physicochemical phenomenon; all of these crucial insights were strongly and sometimes viciously resisted, because the dominant religion of the time happened to think otherwise. Giordano Bruno was burned at the stake for urging the first view; Galileo was forced by threat of torture in the Vatican's basement to recant the second view; the firm belief that disease was a punishment visited by the Devil allowed public health practices that brought chronic plagues to most of the cities of Europe; and the age of the earth and the evolution of life were forced to fight an uphill battle against religious prejudice even in an age of supposed enlightenment.

History aside, the almost universal opinion that one's own religious convictions are the reasoned outcome of a dispassionate evaluation of all of the major alternatives is almost demonstrably false for humanity in general. If that really were the genesis of most people's convictions, then one would expect the major faiths to be distributed more or less randomly or evenly over the globe. But in fact they show a very strong tendency to cluster: Christianity is centered in Europe and the Americas, Islam in Africa and the Middle East, Hinduism in India, and Buddhism in the Orient. Which illustrates what we all suspected anyway: that *social forces* are the primary determinants of religious belief for people in general. To decide scientific questions by appeal to religious orthodoxy would therefore be to put social forces in place of empirical evidence. For all of these reasons, professional scientists and philosophers concerned with the nature of mind generally do their best to keep religious appeals out of the discussion entirely.

The argument from introspection is a much more interesting argument, since it tries to appeal to the direct experience of everyman. But the argument is deeply suspect, in that it assumes that our faculty of inner observation or introspection reveals things as they really are in their innermost nature. This assumption is suspect because we already know that our other forms of observation—sight, hearing, touch, and so on—do no such thing. The red surface of an apple does not *look* like a matrix of molecules reflecting photons at certain critical wavelengths, but that is what it is. The sound of a flute does not *sound* like a sinusoidal compression wave train in the atmosphere, but that is what it is. The warmth of the summer air does not *feel* like the mean kinetic energy of millions of tiny molecules, but that is what it is. If one's pains and hopes and beliefs do not *introspectively* seem like electrochemical states in a neural network, that may be only because our faculty of introspection, like our other senses, is not sufficiently penetrating to reveal such hidden details. Which is just what one would expect anyway. The argument from introspection is therefore entirely without force, unless we can somehow argue that the faculty of introspection is quite different from all other forms of observation.

The argument from irreducibility presents a more serious challenge, but here also its force is less than first impression suggests. Consider first our capacity for mathematical reasoning which so impressed Descartes. The last ten years have made available, to anyone with fifty dollars to spend, electronic calculators whose capacity for mathematical reasoning—the calculational part, at least—far surpasses that of any normal human. The fact is, in the centuries since Descartes' writings, philosophers, logicians, mathematicians, and computer scientists have managed to isolate the general principles of mathematical reasoning, and electronics engineers have created machines that compute in accord with those principles. The result is a hand-held object that would have astonished Descartes. This outcome is impressive not just because machines have proved capable of some of the capacities boasted by human reason, but because some of those achievements invade areas of human reason that past dualistic philosophers have held up as forever closed to mere physical devices.

Although debate on the matter remains open, Descartes' argument from language use is equally dubious. The notion of a *computer language* is by now a commonplace: consider BASIC, PASCAL, FORTRAN, APL, LISP, and so on. Granted, these artificial 'languages' are much simpler in structure and content than human natural language, but the differences may be differences only of degree, and not of kind. As well, the theoretical work of Noam Chomsky and the generative grammar approach to linguistics have done a great deal to explain the human capacity for language use in terms that invite simulation by computers. I do not mean to suggest that truly conversational computers are just around the corner. We have a great deal yet to learn, and fundamental problems yet to solve (mostly having to do with our capacity for inductive or theoretical reasoning). But recent progress here does nothing to support the claim that language use must be forever impossible for a purely physical system. On the contrary, such a claim now appears rather arbitrary and dogmatic, as we shall see in chapter 6.

The next issue is also a live problem: How can we possibly hope to explain or to predict the intrinsic qualities of our sensations, or the meaningful content of our beliefs and desires, in purely physical terms? This is a major challenge to the materialist. But as we shall see in later sections, active research programs are already under way on both problems, and positive suggestions are being explored. It is in fact not impossible to imagine how such explanations might go, though the materialist cannot yet pretend to have solved either problem. Until he does, the dualist will retain a bargaining chip here, but that is about all. What the dualists need in order to establish their case is the conclusion that a physical reduction is outright impossible, and that is a conclusion they have failed to establish. Rhetorical questions, like the one that opens this paragraph, do not constitute arguments. And it is equally difficult, note, to imagine how the relevant phenomena could be explained or predicted solely in terms of the substance dualist's nonphysical mind-stuff. The explanatory problem here is a major challenge to everybody, not just to the materialist. On this issue then, we have a rough standoff.

The final argument in support of dualism urged the existence of parapsychological phenomena such as telepathy and telekinesis, the point being that such mental phenomena are (a) real, and (b) beyond purely physical explanation. This argument is really another instance of the argument from irreducibility discussed above, and as before, it is not entirely clear that such phenomena, even if real, must forever escape a purely physical explanation. The materialist can already suggest a possible mechanism for telepathy, for example. On his view, thinking is an electrical activity within the brain. But according to electromagnetic theory, such changing motions of electric charges must produce electromagnetic waves radiating at the speed of light in all directions, waves that will contain information about the electrical activity that produced them. Such waves can subsequently have effects on the electrical activity of other brains, that is, on their thinking. Call this the 'radio transmitter/ receiver' theory of telepathy.

I do not for a moment suggest that this theory is true: the electromagnetic waves emitted by the brain are fantastically weak (billions of times weaker than the ever present background electromagnetic flux produced by commercial radio stations), and they are almost certain to be hopelessly jumbled together as well. This is one reason why, in the absence of systematic, compelling, and repeatable evidence for the existence of telepathy, one must doubt its possibility. But it is significant that the materialist has the theoretical resources to suggest a detailed possible explanation of telepathy, if it were real, which is more than any dualist has so far done. It is not at all clear, then, that the materialist *must* be at an explanatory disadvantage in these matters. Quite the reverse.

Put the preceding aside, if you wish, for the main difficulty with the argument from parapsychological phenomena is much, much simpler. Despite the endless pronouncements and anecdotes in the popular press, and despite a steady trickle of serious research on such things, there is no significant or trustworthy evidence that such phenomena even exist. The wide gap between popular conviction on this matter, and the actual evidence, is something that itself calls for research. For there is not a single parapsychological effect that can be repeatedly or reliably produced in any laboratory suitably equipped to perform and control the experiment. Not one. Honest researchers have been repeatedly hoodwinked by 'psychic' charlatans with skills derived from the magician's trade, and the history of the subject is largely a history of gullibility, selection of evidence, poor experimental controls, and outright fraud by the occasional researcher as well. If someone really does discover a repeatable parapsychological effect, then we shall have to reevaluate the situation, but as things stand, there is nothing here to support a dualist theory of mind.

Upon critical examination, the arguments in support of dualism lose much of their force. But we are not yet done: there are arguments against dualism, and these also require examination.

Arguments against Dualism   The first argument against dualism urged by the materialists appeals to the greater *simplicity* of their view. It is a principle of rational methodology that, if all else is equal, the simpler of two competing hypotheses should be preferred. This principle is sometimes called "Ockham's Razor"—after William of Ockham, the medieval philosopher who first enunciated it—and it can also be expressed as follows: "Do not multiply entities beyond what is strictly necessary to explain the phenomena." The materialist postulates only one kind of substance (physical matter), and one class of properties (physical properties), whereas the dualist postulates two kinds of matter and/or two classes of properties. And to no explanatory advantage, charges the materialist.

This is not yet a decisive point against dualism, since neither dualism nor materialism can yet explain all of the phenomena to be explained. But the objection does have some force, especially since there is no doubt at all that physical matter exists, while spiritual matter remains a tenuous hypothesis.

If this latter hypothesis brought us some definite explanatory advantage obtainable in no other way, then we would happily violate the demand for simplicity, and we would be right to do so. But it does not, claims the materialist. In fact, the advantage is just the other way around, he argues, and this brings us to the second objection to dualism: the relative *explanatory impotence* of dualism as compared to materialism.

Consider, very briefly, the explanatory resources already available to the neurosciences. We know that the brain exists and what it is made of. We know much of its microstructure: how the neurons are organized into systems and how distinct systems are connected to one another, to the motor nerves going out to the muscles, and to the sensory nerves coming in from the sense organs. We know much of their microchemistry: how the nerve cells fire tiny electrochemical pulses along their various fibers, and how they make other cells fire also, or cease firing. We know some of how such activity processes sensory information, selecting salient or subtle bits to be sent on to higher systems. And we know some of how such activity initiates and coordinates bodily behavior. Thanks mainly to neurology (the branch of medicine concerned with brain pathology), we know a great deal about the correlations between damage to various parts of the human brain, and various behavioral and cognitive deficits from which the victims suffer. There are a great many isolated deficits—some gross, some subtle—that are familiar to neurologists (inability to speak, or to read, or to understand speech, or to recognize faces, or to add/subtract, or to move a certain limb, or to put information into long-term memory, and so on), and their appearance is closely tied to the occurrence of damage to very specific parts of the brain.

Nor are we limited to cataloguing traumas. The growth and development of the brain's microstructure is also something that neuroscience has explored, and such development appears to be the basis of various kinds of learning by the organism. Learning, that is, involves lasting chemical and physical changes in the brain. In sum, the neuroscientist can tell us a great deal about the brain, about its constitution and the physical laws that govern it; he can already explain much of our behavior in terms of the physical, chemical, and electrical properties of the brain; and he has the theoretical resources available to explain a good deal more as our explorations continue. (We shall take a closer look at neurophysiology and neuropsychology in chapter 7.)

Compare now what the neuroscientist can tell us about the brain, and what he can do with that knowledge, with what the dualist can tell us about spiritual substance, and what he can do with those assumptions. Can the dualist tell us anything about the internal constitution of mind-stuff? Of the nonmaterial elements that make it up? Of the laws that govern their behavior? Of the mind's structural connections with the body? Of the manner of its operations? Can he explain human capacities and pathologies in terms of its structures and its defects? The fact is, the dualist can do none of these things, because no detailed theory of mind-stuff has ever been formulated. Compared to the rich resources and explanatory successes of current materialism, dualism is less a theory of mind than it is an empty space waiting for a genuine theory of mind to be put in it.

Thus argues the materialist. But again, this is not a completely decisive point against dualism. The dualist can admit that the brain plays a major role in the administration of both perception and behavior—on his view the brain is the *mediator* between the mind and the body—but he may attempt to argue that the materialist's current successes and future explanatory prospects concern only the mediative functions of the brain, not the *central* capacities of the nonphysical mind, capacities such as reason, emotion, and consciousness itself. On these latter topics, he may argue, both dualism *and* materialism currently draw a blank.

But this reply is not a very good one. So far as the capacity for reasoning is concerned, machines already exist that execute in minutes sophisticated deductive and mathematical calculations that would take a human a lifetime to execute. And so far as the other two mental capacities are concerned, studies of such things as depression, motivation, attention, and sleep have revealed many interesting and puzzling facts about the neurochemical and neurodynamical basis of both emotion and consciousness. The *central* capacities, no less than the peripheral, have been addressed with profit by various materialist research programs.

In any case, the (substance) dualist's attempt to draw a sharp distinction between the unique 'mental' capacities proper to the nonmaterial mind, and the merely mediative capacities of the brain, prompts an argument that comes close to being an outright refutation of (substance) dualism. If there really is a distinct entity in which reasoning, emotion, and consciousness take place, and if that entity is dependent on the brain for nothing more than sensory experiences as input and volitional executions as output, *then one would expect reason, emotion, and consciousness to be relatively invulnerable to direct control or pathology by manipulation or damage to the brain.* But in fact the exact opposite is true. Alcohol, narcotics, or senile degeneration of nerve tissue will impair, cripple, or even destroy one's capacity for rational thought. Psychiatry knows of hundreds of emotion-controlling chemicals (lithium, chlorpromazine, amphetamine, cocaine, and so on) that do their work when vectored into the brain. And the vulnerability of consciousness to the anesthetics, to caffeine, and to something as simple as a sharp blow to the head, shows its very close dependence on neural activity in the brain. All of this makes perfect sense if reason, emotion, and consciousness are activities of the brain itself. But it makes very little sense if they are activities of something else entirely.

We may call this the argument from the *neural dependence* of all known mental phenomena. Property dualism, note, is not threatened by this argument, since, like materialism, property dualism reckons the brain as the seat of all mental activity. We shall conclude this section, however, with an argument that cuts against both varieties of dualism: the argument from *evolutionary history.*

What is the origin of a complex and sophisticated species such as ours? What, for that matter, is the origin of the dolphin, the mouse, or the housefly? Thanks to the fossil record, comparative anatomy, and the biochemistry of proteins and nucleic acids, there is no longer any significant doubt on this matter. Each existing species is a surviving type from a number of variations on an earlier type of organism; each earlier type is in turn a surviving type from a number of variations on a still earlier type of organism; and so on down the branches of the evolutionary tree until, some three billion years ago, we find a trunk of just one or a handful of very simple organisms. These organisms, like their more complex offspring, are just self-repairing, self-replicating, energy-driven molecular structures. (That evolutionary trunk has its own roots in an earlier era of purely chemical evolution, in which the molecular elements of life were themselves pieced together.) The mechanism of development that has structured this tree has two main elements: (1) the occasional blind variation in types of reproducing creature, and (2) the selective survival of some of these types due to the relative reproductive advantage enjoyed by individuals of those types. Over periods of geological time, such a process can produce an enormous variety of organisms, some of them very complex indeed.

For purposes of our discussion, the important point about the standard evolutionary story is that the human species and all of its features are the wholly physical outcome of a purely physical process. Like all but the simplest of organisms, we have a nervous system. And for the same reason: a nervous system permits the discriminative guidance of behavior. But a nervous system is just an active matrix of cells, and a cell is just an active matrix of molecules. We are notable only in that our nervous system is more complex and powerful than those of our fellow creatures. Our inner nature differs from that of simpler creatures in degree, but not in kind.

If this is the correct account of our origins, then there seems neither need, nor room, to fit any nonphysical substances or properties into our theoretical account of ourselves. We are creatures of matter. And we should learn to live with that fact.

wait a minute!

Arguments like these have moved most (but not all) of the professional community to embrace some form of materialism. This has not produced much unanimity, however, since the differences between the several materialist positions are even wider than the differences that divide dualism. The next four sections explore these more recent positions.

What about phenomenology

Suggested Readings

On Substance Dualism

Descartes, René, *The Meditations*, meditation II.
Descartes, René, *Discourse on Method*, part 5.
Eccles, Sir John C., *The Self and Its Brain*, with Sir Karl Popper (New York: Springer-Verlag, 1977).

What about property dualism?

On Property Dualism

Popper, Sir Karl, *The Self and Its Brain,* with Sir John C. Eccles (New York: Springer-Verlag, 1977).

Margolis, Joseph, *Persons and Minds: The Prospects of Nonreductive Materialism* (Dordrecht-Holland: Reidel, 1978).

Jackson, Frank, "Epiphenomenal Qualia," *The Philosophical Quarterly,* vol. 32, no. 127 (April, 1982).

Nagel, Thomas, "What Is It Like to Be a Bat?" *Philosophical Review,* vol. LXXXIII (1974). Reprinted in *Readings in Philosophy of Psychology,* vol. I, ed. N. Block (Cambridge, MA: Harvard University Press, 1980).

2. Philosophical Behaviorism

Philosophical behaviorism reached the peak of its influence during the first and second decades after World War II. It was jointly motivated by at least three intellectual fashions. The first motivation was a reaction against dualism. The second motivation was the Logical Positivists' idea that the meaning of any sentence was ultimately a matter of the observable circumstances that would tend to verify or confirm that sentence. And the third motivation was a general assumption that most, if not all, philosophical problems are the result of linguistic or conceptual confusion, and are to be solved (or dissolved) by careful analysis of the language in which the problem is expressed.

In fact, philosophical behaviorism is not so much a theory about what mental states are (in their inner nature) as it is a theory about how to analyze or to understand the vocabulary we use to talk about them. Specifically, the claim is that talk about emotions and sensations and beliefs and desires is not talk about ghostly inner episodes, but is rather a shorthand way of talking about actual and potential patterns of *behavior*. In its strongest and most straightforward form, philosophical behaviorism claims that any sentence about a mental state can be paraphrased, without loss of meaning, into a long and complex sentence about what observable behavior *would* result if the person in question were in this, that, or the other observable circumstance.

A helpful analogy here is the dispositional property, *being soluble*. To say that a sugar cube is soluble is not to say that the sugar cube enjoys some ghostly inner state. It is just to say that *if* the sugar cube were put in water, then it *would* dissolve. More strictly,

"*x* is water soluble"

is equivalent by definition to

"if *x* were put in unsaturated water, *x* would dissolve."

This is one example of what is called an "operational definition". The term "soluble" is defined in terms of certain operations or tests that would reveal whether or not the term actually applies in the case to be tested.

According to the behaviorist, a similar analysis holds for mental states such as "wants a Caribbean holiday", save that the analysis is much richer. To say that Anne wants a Caribbean holiday is to say that (1) if asked whether that is what she wants, she would answer yes, and (2) if given new holiday brochures for Jamaica and Japan, she would peruse the ones for Jamaica first, and (3) if given a ticket on this Friday's flight to Jamaica, she would go, and so on and so on.

Unlike solubility, claims the behaviorist, most mental states are *multi-tracked* dispositions. But dispositions they remain.

There is therefore no point in worrying about the 'relation' between the mind and the body, on this view. To talk about Marie Curie's mind, for example, is not to talk about some 'thing' that she 'possesses'; it is to talk about certain of her extraordinary capacities and dispositions. The mind-body problem, concludes the behaviorist, is a pseudoproblem.

Behaviorism is clearly consistent with a materialist conception of human beings. Material objects can have dispositional properties, even multitracked ones, so there is no necessity to embrace dualism to make sense of our psychological vocabulary. (It should be pointed out, however, that behaviorism is strictly consistent with dualism also. Even if philosophical behaviorism were true, it would remain possible that our multitracked dispositions are grounded in immaterial mind-stuff rather than in molecular structures. This is not a possibility that most behaviorists took seriously, however, for the many reasons outlined at the end of the preceding section.)

Philosophical behaviorism, unfortunately, had two major flaws that made it awkward to believe, even for its defenders. It evidently ignored, and even denied, the 'inner' aspect of our mental states. To have a pain, for example, seems to be not merely a matter of being inclined to moan, to wince, to take aspirin, and so on. Pains also have an intrinsic qualitative nature (a horrible one) that is revealed in introspection, and any theory of mind that ignores or denies such *qualia* is simply derelict in its duty.

This problem received much attention from behaviorists, and serious attempts were made to solve it. The details take us deeply into semantical problems, however, so we shall postpone further discussion of this difficulty until chapter 3.

The second flaw emerged when behaviorists attempted to specify in detail the multitracked disposition said to constitute any given mental state. The list of conditionals necessary for an adequate analysis of "wants a Caribbean holiday", for example, seemed not just to be long, but to be indefinitely or even infinitely long, with no finite way of specifying the elements to be included. And no term can be well-defined whose *definiens* is open-ended and unspecific in this way. Further, each conditional of the long analysis was suspect on its own. Supposing that Anne does want a Caribbean holiday, conditional (1) above will be true only if she isn't *secretive* about her holiday fantasies; conditional (2) will be true only if she isn't already *bored* with the Jamaica brochures; conditional (3) will be true only if she doesn't *believe* the Friday flight will be hijacked, and so forth. But to repair each conditional by adding in the relevant qualification would be to reintroduce a series of *mental* elements into the business end of the definition, and we would no longer be defining the mental solely in terms of publicly observable circumstances and behavior.

So long as behaviorism seemed the only alternative to dualism, philosophers were prepared to struggle with these flaws in hopes of repairing or defusing them. However, three more materialist theories rose to prominence during the late fifties and sixties, and the flight from behaviorism was swift.

(I close this section with a cautionary note. The *philosophical* behaviorism discussed above is to be sharply distinguished from the *methodological* behaviorism that has enjoyed such a wide influence within psychology. In its bluntest form, this latter view urges that any new theoretical terms invented by the science of psychology *should be* operationally defined, in order to guarantee that psychology maintains a firm contact with empirical reality. Philosophical behaviorism, by contrast, claims that all of the common-sense psychological terms in our prescientific vocabulary *already* get whatever meaning they have from (tacit) operational definitions. The two views are logically distinct, and the methodology might be a wise one, for new theoretical terms, even though the correlative analysis of common-sense mental terms is wrong.)

Suggested Readings

Ryle, Gilbert, *The Concept of Mind* (London: Hutchinson & Company, 1949), chapters I and V.

Malcolm, Norman, "Wittgenstein's *Philosophical Investigations*," *Philosophical Review*, vol. XLVII (1956). Reprinted in *The Philosophy of Mind*, ed. V. C. Chappell (Englewood Cliffs, NJ: Prentice-Hall, 1962).

3. Reductive Materialism (the Identity Theory)

Reductive materialism, more commonly known as *the identity theory,* is the most straightforward of the several materialist theories of mind. Its central claim is simplicity itself: Mental states *are* physical states of the brain. That is, each type of mental state or process is *numerically identical with* (is one and the very same thing as) some type of physical state or process within the brain or central nervous system. At present we do not know enough about the intricate functionings of the brain actually to state the relevant identities, but the identity theory is committed to the idea that brain research will eventually reveal them. (Partly to help us evaluate that claim, we shall examine current brain research in chapter 7.)

Historical Parallels   As the identity theorist sees it, the result here predicted has familiar parallels elsewhere in our scientific history. Consider sound. We now know that sound is just a train of compression waves traveling through the air, and that the property of being high pitched is identical with the property of having a high oscillatory frequency. We have learned that light is just electromagnetic waves, and our best current theory says that the color of an object is identical with a triplet of reflectance efficiencies the object has, rather like a musical chord that it strikes, though the 'notes' are struck in electromagnetic waves instead of in sound waves. We now appreciate that the warmth or coolness of a body is just the energy of motion of the molecules that make it up: warmth is identical with high average molecular kinetic energy, and coolness is identical with low average molecular kinetic energy. We know that lightning is identical with a sudden large-scale discharge of electrons between clouds, or between the atmosphere and the ground. What we now think of as 'mental states,' argues the identity theorist, are identical with brain states in exactly the same way.

Intertheoretic Reduction   These illustrative parallels are all cases of successful *intertheoretic reduction.* That is, they are all cases where a new and very powerful theory turns out to entail a set of propositions and principles that mirror perfectly (or almost perfectly) the propositions and principles of some older theory or conceptual framework. The relevant principles entailed by the new theory have the same structure as the corresponding principles of the old framework, and they apply in exactly the same cases. The only difference is that where the old principles contained (for example) the notions of "heat", "is hot", and "is cold", the new principles contain instead the notions of "total molecular kinetic energy", "has a high mean molecular kinetic energy", and "has a low mean molecular kinetic energy".

If the new framework is far better than the old at explaining and predicting phenomena, then we have excellent reason for believing that the theoretical terms of the *new* framework are the terms that describe reality correctly. But if the old framework worked adequately, so far as it went, and if it parallels a portion of the new theory in the systematic way described, then we may properly conclude that the old terms and the new terms refer to the very same things, or express the very same properties. We conclude that we have apprehended the very same reality that is incompletely described by the old framework, but with a new and more penetrating conceptual framework. And we announce what philosophers of science call "intertheoretic identities": light *is* electromagnetic waves, temperature *is* mean molecular kinetic energy, and so forth.

The examples of the preceding two paragraphs share one more important feature in common. They are all cases where the things or properties on the receiving end of the reduction are *observable* things and properties within our *common-sense* conceptual framework. They show that intertheoretic reduction occurs not only between conceptual frameworks in the theoretical stratosphere: common-sense observables can also be reduced. There would therefore be nothing particularly surprising about a reduction of our familiar introspectible mental states to physical states of the brain. All that would be required would be that an explanatorily successful neuroscience develop to the point where it entails a suitable 'mirror image' of the assumptions and principles that constitute our common-sense conceptual framework for mental states, an image where brain-state terms occupy the positions held by mental-state terms in the assumptions and principles of common sense. If this (rather demanding) condition were indeed met, then, as in the historical cases cited, we would be justified in announcing a reduction, and in asserting the identity of mental states with brain states.

Arguments for the Identity Theory

What reasons does the identity theorist have for believing that neuroscience will eventually achieve the strong conditions necessary for the reduction of our 'folk' psychology? There are at least four reasons, all directed at the conclusion that the correct account of human-behavior-and-its-causes must reside in the physical neurosciences.

We can point first to the purely physical origins and ostensibly physical constitution of each individual human. One begins as a genetically programmed monocellular organization of molecules (a fertilized ovum), and one develops from there by the accretion of further molecules whose structure and integration is controlled by the information coded in the DNA molecules of the cell nucleus. The result of such a process would be a purely physical system whose behavior arises from its internal operations and its interactions with the rest of the physical world. And those behavior-controlling internal operations are precisely what the neurosciences are about.

This argument coheres with a second argument. The origins of each *type* of animal also appear exhaustively physical in nature. The argument from evolutionary history discussed earlier (p. 20) lends further support to the identity theorist's claim, since evolutionary theory provides the only serious explanation we have for the behavior-controlling capacities of the brain and central nervous system. Those systems were selected for because of the many advantages (ultimately, the reproductive advantage) held by creatures whose behavior was thus controlled. Again our behavior appears to have its basic causes in neural activity.

The identity theorist finds further support in the argument, discussed earlier, from the neural dependence of all known mental phenomena (see p. 20). This is precisely what one should expect, if the identity theory is true. Of course, systematic neural dependence is also a consequence of property dualism, but here the identity theorist will appeal to considerations of simplicity. Why admit two radically different classes of properties and operations if the explanatory job can be done by one?

A final argument derives from the growing success of the neurosciences in unraveling the nervous systems of many creatures and in explaining their behavioral capacities and deficits in terms of the structures discovered. The preceding arguments all suggest that neuroscience should be successful in this endeavor, and the fact is that the continuing history of neuroscience bears them out. Especially in the case of very simple creatures (as one would expect), progress has been rapid. And progress has also been made with humans, though for obvious moral reasons exploration must be more cautious and circumspect. In sum, the neurosciences have a long way to go, but progress to date provides substantial encouragement to the identity theorist.

Even so, these arguments are far from decisive in favor of the identity theory. No doubt they do provide an overwhelming case for the idea that the causes of human and animal behavior are essentially physical in nature, but the identity theory claims more than just this. It claims that neuroscience will discover a taxonomy of neural states that stand in a one-to-one correspondence with the mental states of our common-sense taxonomy. Claims for intertheoretic identity will be justified only if such a match-up can be found. But nothing in the preceding arguments guarantees that the old and new frameworks will match up in this way, even if the new framework is a roaring success at explaining and predicting our behavior. Furthermore, there are arguments from other positions within the materialist camp to the effect that such convenient match-ups are rather unlikely. Before exploring those, however, let us look at some more traditional objections to the identity theory.

Arguments against the Identity Theory   We may begin with the argument from introspection discussed earlier. Introspection reveals a domain of thoughts, sensations, and emotions, not a domain of electrochemical impulses in a neural network. Mental states and properties, as revealed in introspection, appear radically different from any neurophysiological states and properties. How could they possibly be the very same things?

The answer, as we have already seen, is, "Easily." In discriminating red from blue, sweet from sour, and hot from cold, our external senses are actually discriminating between subtle differences in intricate electromagnetic, stereochemical, and micromechanical properties of physical objects. But our senses are not sufficiently penetrating to reveal on their own the detailed nature of those intricate properties. That requires theoretical research and experimental exploration with specially designed instruments. The same is presumably true of our 'inner' sense: introspection. It may discriminate efficiently between a great variety of neural states, without being able to reveal on its own the detailed nature of the states being discriminated. Indeed, it would be faintly miraculous if it did reveal them, just as miraculous as if unaided sight were to reveal the existence of interacting electric and magnetic fields whizzing by with an oscillatory frequency of a million billion hertz and a wavelength of less than a millionth of a meter. For despite 'appearances', that is what light is. The argument from introspection, therefore, is quite without force.

The next objection argues that the identification of mental states with brain states would commit us to statements that are literally unintelligible, to what philosophers have called "category errors", and that the identification is therefore a case of sheer conceptual confusion. We may begin the discussion by noting a most important law concerning numerical identity. Leibniz' Law states that two items are numerically identical just in case any property had by either one of them is also had by the other: in logical notation,

$$(x)(y)[(x = y) \equiv (F)(Fx \equiv Fy)].$$

This law suggests a way of refuting the identity theory: find some property that is true of brain states, but not of mental states (or vice versa), and the theory would be exploded.

Spatial properties were often cited to this end. Brain states and processes must of course have some specific spatial location: in the brain as a whole, or in some part of it. And if mental states are identical with brain states, then they must have the very same spatial location. But it is literally meaningless, runs the argument, to say that my feeling-of-pain is located in my ventral thalamus, or that my belief-that-the-sun-is-a-star is located in the temporal lobe of my left cerebral hemisphere. Such claims are as meaningless as the claim that the number 5 is green, or that love weighs twenty grams.

Trying the same move from the other direction, some have argued that it is senseless to ascribe the various *semantic* properties to brain states. Our thoughts and beliefs, for example, have a meaning, a specific propositional content; they are either true or false; and they can enjoy relations such as consistency and entailment. If thoughts and beliefs were brain states, then all these semantic properties would have to be true of brain states. But it is senseless, runs the argument, to say that some resonance in my association cortex is true, or logically entails some other resonance close by, or has the meaning that *P*.

Neither of these moves has the same bite it did twenty years ago, since familiarity with the identity theory and growing awareness of the brain's role have tended to reduce the feelings of semantic oddity produced by the claims at issue. But even if they still struck all of us as semantically confused, this would carry little weight. The claim that sound has a wavelength, or that light has a frequency, must have seemed equally unintelligible in advance of the conviction that both sound and light are wave phenomena. (See, for example, Bishop Berkeley's eighteenth-century dismissal of the idea that sound is a vibratory motion of the air, in Dialogue I of his *Three Dialogues*. The objections are voiced by Philonous.) The claim that warmth is measured in kilogram·meters^2/seconds^2 would have seemed semantically perverse before we understood that temperature is mean molecular kinetic energy. And Copernicus' sixteenth-century claim that the earth *moves* also struck people as absurd to the point of perversity. It is not difficult to appreciate why. Consider the following argument.

> Copernicus' claim that the earth moves is sheer conceptual confusion. For consider what it *means* to say that something moves: "*x* moves" means "*x* changes position relative to the earth." Thus, to say that the earth moves is to say that the earth changes position relative to itself! Which is absurd. Copernicus' position is therefore an abuse of language.

The *meaning analysis* here invoked might well have been correct, but all that would have meant is that the speaker should have set about changing his meanings. The fact is, any language involves a rich network of assumptions about the structure of the world, and if a sentence S provokes intuitions of semantic oddness, that is usually because S violates one or more of those background assumptions. But one cannot always reject S for that reason alone, since the overthrow of those background assumptions may be precisely what the facts require. The 'abuse' of accepted modes of speech is often an essential feature of real scientific progress! Perhaps we shall just have to get used to the idea that mental states have anatomical locations and brain states have semantic properties.

While the charge of sheer senselessness can be put aside, the identity theorist does owe us some account of exactly how physical brain states can have semantic properties. The account currently being explored can be outlined as follows. Let us begin by asking how it is that a particular *sentence* (= utterance type) has the specific propositional content it has: the sentence "La pomme est rouge", for example. Note first that a sentence is always an integrated part of an entire system of sentences: a language. Any given sentence enjoys many relations with countless other sentences: it entails many sentences, is entailed by many others, is consistent with some, is inconsistent with others, provides confirming evidence for yet others, and so forth. And speakers who use that sentence within that language draw inferences in accordance with those relations. Evidently, each sentence (or each set of equivalent sentences) enjoys a unique pattern of such entailment relations: it plays a distinct inferential role in a complex linguistic economy. Accordingly, we say that the sentence "La pomme est rouge" has the propositional content, *the apple is red*, because the sentence "La pomme est rouge" plays *the same role* in French that the sentence "The apple is red" plays in English. To have the relevant propositional content is just to play the relevant inferential role in a cognitive economy.

Returning now to types of brain states, there is no problem in principle in assuming that one's brain is the seat of a complex inferential economy in which types of brain states are the role-playing elements. According to the theory of meaning just sketched, such states would then have propositional content, since having content is not a matter of whether the contentful item is a pattern of sound, a pattern of letters on paper, a set of raised Braille bumps, or a pattern of neural activity. What matters is the inferential role the item plays. Propositional content, therefore, seems within the reach of brain states after all.

We began this subsection with an argument against materialism that appealed to the qualitative *nature* of our mental states, as revealed in introspection. The next argument appeals to the simple fact that they are introspectible at all.

1. My mental states are introspectively known by me as states of my conscious self.

2. My brain states are *not* introspectively known by me as states of my conscious self.

Therefore, by Leibniz' Law (that numerically identical things must have exactly the same properties),

3. My mental states are not identical with my brain states.

This, in my experience, is the most beguiling form of the argument from introspection, seductive of freshmen and faculty alike. But it is a straightforward instance of a well-known fallacy, which is clearly illustrated in the following parallel arguments:

1. Muhammad Ali is widely known as a heavyweight champion.

2. Cassius Clay is *not* widely known as a heavyweight champion.

Therefore, by Leibniz' Law,

3. Muhammad Ali is not identical with Cassius Clay.

or,

1. Aspirin is recognized by John to be a pain reliever.

2. Acetylsalicylic acid is *not* recogized by John to be a pain reliever.

Therefore, by Leibniz' Law,

3. Aspirin is not identical with acetylsalicylic acid.

Despite the truth of the relevant premises, both conclusions are false: the identities are wholly genuine. Which means that both arguments are invalid. The problem is that the 'property' ascribed in premise (1), and withheld in premise (2), consists only in the subject item's being *recognized, perceived,* or *known* as something-or-other. But such apprehension is not a genuine property of the item itself, fit for divining identities, since one and the same subject may be successfully recognized under one name or description, and yet fail to be recognized under another (accurate, coreferential) description. Bluntly, Leibniz' Law is not valid for these bogus 'properties'. The attempt to use them as above commits what logicians call an *intensional* fallacy. The premises may reflect, not the failure of certain objective identities, but only our continuing failure to appreciate them.

A different version of the preceding argument must also be considered, since it may be urged that one's brain states are more than merely not (yet) known by introspection: they are not know*able* by introspection under any circumstances. Thus,

1. My mental states are knowable by introspection.

2. My brain states are *not* knowable by introspection.

Therefore, by Leibniz' Law,

3. My mental states are not identical with my brain states.

Here the critic will insist that being know*able* by introspection *is* a genuine property of a thing, and that this modified version of the argument is free of the 'intensional fallacy' discussed above.

And so it is. But now the materialist is in a position to insist that the argument contains a false premise—premise (2). For if mental states are indeed brain states, then it is really brain states we have been introspecting all along, though without fully appreciating what they are. And if we can learn to think of and recognize those states under mentalistic descriptions, as we all have, then we can certainly learn to think of and recognize them under their more penetrating neuro-physiological descriptions. At the very least, premise (2) simply begs the question against the identity theorist. The mistake is amply illustrated in the following parallel argument:

1. Temperature is knowable by feeling.

2. Mean molecular kinetic energy is *not* knowable by feeling.

Therefore, by Leibniz' Law,

3. Temperature is not identical with mean molecular kinetic energy.

This identity, at least, is long established, and this argument is certainly unsound: premise (2) is false. Just as one can learn to feel that the summer air is about 70°F, or 21°C, so one can learn to feel that the mean KE of its molecules is about 6.2×10^{-21} joules, for whether we realize it or not, that is what our discriminatory mechanisms are keyed to. Perhaps our brain states are similarly accessible. The introspectibility of brain states is addressed again in chapter 8.

Consider now a final argument, again based on the introspectible qualities of our sensations. Imagine a future neuroscientist who comes to know everything there is to know about the physical structure and activity of the brain and its visual system, of its actual and possible states. If for some reason she has never actually *had* a sensation-of-red (because of color blindness, say, or an unusual environment), then there will remain something she does *not* know about certain sensations: *what it is like to have a sensation-of-red*. Therefore, complete knowledge of the physical facts of visual perception and its related brain activity still leaves something out. Accordingly, materialism cannot give an adequate account of all mental phenomena, and the identity theory must be false.

The identity theorist can reply that this argument exploits an unwitting equivocation on the term "know". Concerning our neuroscientist's utopian knowledge of the brain, "knows" means something like "has mastered the relevant set of neuroscientific propositions". Concerning her (missing) knowledge of what it is like to have a sensation-of-red, "knows" means something like "has a prelinguistic representation of redness in her mechanisms for noninferential discrimination". It is true that one might have the former without the latter, but the materialist is not committed to the idea that having knowledge in the former sense automatically constitutes having knowledge in the second sense. The identity theorist can admit a duality, or even a plurality, of different *types of knowledge* without thereby committing himself to a duality in *types of things known*. The difference between a person who knows all about the visual cortex but has never enjoyed the sensation-of-red, and a person who knows no neuroscience but knows well the sensation-of-red, may reside not in *what* is respectively known by each (brain states by the former, nonphysical *qualia* by the latter), but rather in the different *type*, or *medium*, or *level* of representation each has of exactly the same thing: brain states.

In sum, there are pretty clearly more ways of 'having knowledge' than just having mastered a set of sentences, and the materialist can freely admit that one has 'knowledge' of one's sensations in a way that is independent of the neuroscience one may have learned. Animals, including humans, presumably have a prelinguistic mode of sensory representation. This does not mean that sensations are beyond the reach of physical science. *It just means that the brain uses more modes and media of representation than the mere storage of sentences.* All the identity theorist needs to claim is that those other modes of representation will also yield to neuroscientific explanation.

The identity theory has proved to be very resilient in the face of these predominantly antimaterialist objections. But further objections, rooted in competing forms of materialism, constitute a much more serious threat, as the following sections will show.

Suggested Readings

On the Identity Theory

Feigl, Herbert, "The Mind-Body Problem: *Not* a Pseudo-Problem," in *Dimensions of Mind*, ed. Sidney Hook (New York: New York University Press, 1960).

Place, U. T., "Is Consciousness a Brain Process?" *British Journal of Psychology*, vol. XLVII

(1956). Reprinted in *The Philosophy of Mind*, ed. V. C. Chappell (Englewood Cliffs, NJ: Prentice-Hall, 1962).

Smart, J. J. C., "Sensations and Brain Processes," *Philosophical Review*, vol. LXVIII (1959). Reprinted in *The Philosophy of Mind*, ed. V. C. Chappell (Englewood Cliffs, NJ: Prentice-Hall, 1962).

Lewis, David, "An Argument for the Identity Theory," *The Journal of Philosophy*, vol. LXIII, no. 1 (1966).

Nagel, Thomas, "What Is It Like to Be a Bat?" *Philosophical Review*, vol. LXXXIII (1974). Reprinted in *Readings in Philosophy of Psychology*, vol. I, ed. N. Block (Cambridge, MA: Harvard University Press, 1980).

Jackson, Frank, "Epiphenomenal Qualia," *The Philosophical Quarterly*, vol. 32, no. 127 (April, 1982).

Churchland, Paul, "Reduction, Qualia, and the Direct Introspection of Brain States," *Journal of Philosophy*, vol. LXXXII, no. 1 (1985).

Jackson, Frank, "What Mary Didn't Know," *Journal of Philosophy*, vol. LXXXIII, no. 5 (1986).

Churchland, Paul, "Some Reductive Strategies in Cognitive Neurobiology," *Mind*, vol. 95, no. 379 (1986).

On Intertheoretic Reduction

Nagel, Ernst, *The Structure of Science* (New York: Harcourt, Brace, & World, 1961), chapter 11.

Feyerabend, Paul, "Explanation, Reduction, and Empiricism," in *Minnesota Studies in the Philosophy of Science*, vol. III, eds. H. Feigl and G. Maxwell (Minneapolis: University of Minnesota Press, 1962).

Churchland, Paul, *Scientific Realism and the Plasticity of Mind* (Cambridge: Cambridge University Press, 1979), chapter 3, section 11.

Hooker, Clifford, "Towards a General Theory of Reduction," *Dialogue*, vol. XX, nos. 1–3 (1981).

4. Functionalism

According to *functionalism*, the essential or defining feature of any type of mental state is the set of causal relations it bears to (1) environmental effects on the body, (2) other types of mental states, and (3) bodily behavior. Pain, for example, characteristically results from some bodily damage or trauma; it causes distress, annoyance, and practical reasoning aimed at relief; and it causes wincing, blanching, and nursing of the traumatized area. Any state that plays exactly that functional role is a pain, according to functionalism. Similarly, other types of mental states (sensations, fears, beliefs, and so on) are also defined by their unique causal roles in a complex economy of internal states mediating sensory inputs and behavioral outputs.

This view may remind the reader of behaviorism, and indeed it is the heir to behaviorism, but there is one fundamental difference between the two theories. Where the behaviorist hoped to define each type of mental state solely in terms of environmental input and behavioral output, the functionalist denies that this is possible. As he sees it, the adequate characterization of almost any mental state involves an ineliminable reference to a variety of other mental states with which it is causally connected, and so a reductive definition solely in terms of publicly observable inputs and outputs is quite impossible. Functionalism is therefore immune to one of the main objections against behaviorism.

Thus the difference between functionalism and behaviorism. The difference between functionalism and the identity theory will emerge from the following argument raised against the identity theory.

Imagine a being from another planet, says the functionalist, a being with an alien physiological constitution, a constitution based on the chemical element silicon, for example, instead of on the element carbon, as ours is. The chemistry and even the physical structure of the alien's brain would have to be systematically different from ours. But even so, that alien brain could well sustain a functional economy of internal states whose mutual *relations* parallel perfectly the mutual relations that define our own mental states. The alien may have an internal state that meets all the conditions for being a pain state, as outlined earlier. That state, considered from a purely physical point of view, would have a very different makeup from a human pain state, but it could nevertheless be identical to a human pain state from a purely functional point of view. And so for all of his functional states.

If the alien's functional economy of internal states were indeed *functionally isomorphic* with our own internal economy—if those states were causally connected to inputs, to one another, and to behavior in

ways that parallel our own internal connections—then the alien would
have pains, and desires, and hopes, and fears just as fully as we, despite
the differences in the physical system that sustains or realizes those
functional states. What is important for mentality is not the matter of
which the creature is made, but the structure of the internal activities
which that matter sustains.

If we can think of one alien constitution, we can think of many, and
the point just made can also be made with an artificial system. Were
we to create an electronic system—a computer of some kind—whose
internal economy were functionally isomorphic with our own in all
the relevant ways, then it too would be the subject of mental states.

What this illustrates is that there are almost certainly many more
ways than one for nature, and perhaps even for man, to put together
a thinking, feeling, perceiving creature. And this raises a problem for
the identity theory, for it seems that there is no single type of physical
state to which a given type of mental state must always correspond.
Ironically, there are *too many* different kinds of physical systems that
can realize the functional economy characteristic of conscious intelligence. If we consider the universe at large, therefore, and the future
as well as the present, it seems quite unlikely that the identity theorist
is going to find the one-to-one match-ups between the concepts of our
common-sense mental taxonomy and the concepts of an overarching
theory that encompasses all of the relevant physical systems. But that
is what intertheoretic reduction is standardly said to require. The prospects for universal identities, between types of mental states and types
of brain states, are therefore slim.

If the functionalists reject the traditional 'mental-type = physical
type' identity theory, virtually all of them remain committed to a weaker
'mental token = physical token' identity theory, for they still maintain
that each *instance* of a given type of mental state is numerically identical
with some specific physical state in some physical system or other. It
is only universal (type/type) identities that are rejected. Even so, this
rejection is typically taken to support the claim that the science of
psychology is or should be *methodologically autonomous* from the various
physical sciences such as physics, biology, and even neurophysiology.
Psychology, it is claimed, has its own irreducible laws and its own
abstract subject matter.

As this book is written, functionalism is probably the most widely
held theory of mind among philosophers, cognitive psychologists, and
artificial intelligence researchers. Some of the reasons are apparent
from the preceding discussion, and there are further reasons as well.
In characterizing mental states as essentially functional states, functionalism places the concerns of psychology at a level that abstracts

from the teeming detail of a brain's neurophysiological (or crystallo-graphic, or microelectronic) structure. The science of psychology, it is occasionally said, is methodologically autonomous from those other sciences (biology, neuroscience, circuit theory) whose concerns are with what amount to engineering details. This provides a rationale for a great deal of work in cognitive psychology and artificial intelligence, where researchers postulate a system of abstract functional states and then test the postulated system, often by way of its computer simulation, against human behavior in similar circumstances. The aim of such work is to discover in detail the functional organization that makes us what we are. (Partly in order to evaluate the prospects for a functionalist philosophy of mind, we shall examine some of the recent research in artificial intelligence in chapter 6.)

Arguments against Functionalism   Current popularity aside, function-alism also faces difficulties. The most commonly posed objection cites an old friend: sensory qualia. Functionalism may escape one of behaviorism's fatal flaws, it is said, but it still falls prey to the other. By attempting to make its *relational* properties the definitive feature of any mental state, functionalism ignores the 'inner' or qualitative nature of our mental states. But their qualitative nature is the essential feature of a great many types of mental state (pain, sensations of color, of temperature, of pitch, and so on), runs the objection, and functionalism is therefore false.

The standard illustration of this apparent failing is called "the inverted spectrum thought-experiment". It is entirely conceivable, runs the story, that the range of color sensations that I enjoy upon viewing standard objects is simply inverted relative to the color sensations that you enjoy. When viewing a tomato, I may have what is really a sensation-of-green where you have the normal sensation-of-red; when viewing a banana, I may have what is really sensation-of-blue where you have the normal sensation-of-yellow; and so forth. But since we have no way of com-paring our inner qualia, and since I shall make all the same observational discriminations among objects that you will, there is no way to tell whether my spectrum is inverted relative to yours.

The problem for functionalism arises as follows. Even if my spectrum is inverted relative to yours, we remain functionally isomorphic with one another. My visual sensation upon viewing a tomato is *functionally* identical with your visual sensation upon viewing a tomato. According to functionalism, therefore, they are the very same type of state, and it does not even make sense to suppose that my sensation is 'really' a sensation-of-green. If it meets the functional conditions for being a sensation-of-red, then by definition it is a sensation-of-red. According to functionalism, apparently, a spectrum inversion of the kind described is ruled out by definition. But such inversions are entirely conceivable, concludes the objection, and if functionalism entails that they are not conceivable, then functionalism is false.

Another qualia-related worry for functionalism is the so-called "absent qualia problem". The functional organization characteristic of conscious intelligence can be instantiated (= realized or instanced) in a considerable variety of physical systems, some of them radically different from a normal human. For example, a giant electronic computer might instantiate it, and there are more radical possibilities still. One writer asks us to imagine the people of China—all 10^9 of them—organized into an intricate game of mutual interactions so that collectively they constitute a giant brain which exchanges inputs and outputs with a single robot body. That system of the robot-plus-10^9-unit-brain could presumably instantiate the relevant functional organization (though no doubt it would be much slower in its activities than a human or a computer), and would therefore be the subject of mental states, according to functionalism. But surely, it is urged, the complex states that there play the functional roles of pain, pleasure, and sensations-of-color would not have intrinsic qualia as ours do, and would therefore fail to be genuine mental states. Again, functionalism seems at best an incomplete account of the nature of mental states.

It has recently been argued that both the inverted-qualia and the absent-qualia objections can be met, without violence to functionalism and without significant violence to our common-sense intuitions about qualia. Consider the inversion problem first. I think the functionalist is right to insist that the type-identity of our visual sensations be reckoned according to their functional role. But the objector is also right in insisting that a relative inversion of two people's qualia, without functional inversion, is entirely conceivable. The apparent inconsistency between these positions can be dissolved by insisting that (1) our functional states (or rather, their physical realizations) do indeed have an intrinsic nature on which our introspective identification of those states depends; while also insisting that (2) such intrinsic natures are nevertheless not essential to the type-identity of a given mental state, and may indeed *vary* from instance to instance of the same type of mental state.

What this means is that the qualitative character of your sensation-of-red might be different from the qualitative character of my sensation-of-red, slightly or substantially, and a third person's sensation-of-red might be different again. But so long as all three states are standardly caused by red objects and standardly cause all three of us to believe that something is red, then all three states are sensations-of-red, whatever their intrinsic qualitative character. Such intrinsic qualia merely serve as salient features that permit the quick introspective identification of sensations, as black-on-orange stripes serve as a salient feature for the quick visual identification of tigers. But specific qualia are not essential to the type-identity of mental states, any more than black-on-orange stripes are essential to the type-identity of tigers.

Plainly, this solution requires the functionalist to admit the *reality* of qualia, and we may wonder how there can be room for qualia in his materialist world-picture. Perhaps they can be fit in as follows: *identify* them with physical properties of whatever physical states instantiate the mental (functional) states that display them. For example, identify the qualitative nature of your sensations-of-red with that physical feature (of the brain state that instantiates it) to which your mechanisms of introspective discrimination are in fact responding when you judge that you have a sensation-of-red. If materialism is true, then there must *be* some internal physical feature or other to which your discrimination of sensations-of-red is keyed: *that* is the quale of your sensations-of-red. If the pitch of a sound can turn out to be the frequency of an oscillation in air pressure, there is no reason why the quale of a sensation cannot turn out to be, say, a spiking frequency in a certain neural pathway. (More likely, it will be a peculiar group or *set* of spiking frequencies, as claimed by the *vectorial* or *across-fiber pattern* theory of sensory coding. 'Spikes' are the tiny electrochemical pulses by which our brain cells communicate with each other along the thin fibers that connect them. For more on all of this, see Chapter 7.)

This entails that creatures with a physical constitution different from ours may have qualia different from ours, despite being psychologically isomorphic with us. It does not entail that they *must* have different qualia, however. If the qualitative character of my sensation-of-red is really a spiking frequency of 90 hertz in a certain neural pathway, it is possible that an electromechanical robot might enjoy the very same qualitative character if, in reporting sensations-of-red, the robot were responding to a spiking frequency of 90 hertz in a corresponding *copper* pathway. It might be the spiking frequency that matters to our respective mechanisms of discrimination, not the nature of the medium that carries it.

This proposal also suggests a solution to the absent qualia problem. So long as the physical system at issue is functionally isomorphic with us, to the last detail, then it will be equally capable of subtle introspective discriminations among its sensations. Those discriminations must be made on some systematic physical basis, that is, on some characteristic physical features of the states being discriminated. Those features at the objective focus of the system's discriminatory mechanisms, *those* are its sensory qualia—though the alien system is no more likely to appreciate their true physical nature than we appeciate the true physical nature of our own qualia. Sensory qualia are therefore an inevitable concomitant of any system with the kind of functional organization at issue. It may be difficult or impossible to 'see' the qualia in an alien system, but it is equally difficult to 'see' them even when looking into a human brain.

I leave it to the reader to judge the adequacy of these responses. If they are adequate, then, given its other virtues, functionalism must be conceded a very strong position among the competing contemporary theories of mind. It is interesting, however, that the defense offered in the last paragraph found it necessary to take a leaf from the identity theorist's book (types of quale are reduced to or identified with types of physical state), since the final objection we shall consider also tends to blur the distinction between functionalism and reductive materialism.

Consider the property of *temperature*, runs the objection. Here we have a paradigm of a physical property, one that has also been cited as the paradigm of a successfully *reduced* property, as expressed in the intertheoretic identity

"temperature = mean kinetic energy of constituent molecules".

Strictly speaking, however, this identity is true only for the temperature of a gas, where simple particles are free to move in ballistic fashion. In a *solid*, temperature is realized differently, since the interconnected molecules are confined to a variety of vibrational motions. In a *plasma*, temperature is something else again, since a plasma has no constituent molecules; they, and their constituent atoms, have been ripped to pieces. And even a *vacuum* has a so-called 'blackbody' temperature—in the distribution of electromagnetic waves coursing through it. Here temperature has nothing to do with the kinetic energy of particles.

It is plain that the physical property of temperature enjoys 'multiple instantiations' no less than do psychological properties. Does this mean that thermodynamics (the theory of heat and temperature) is an 'autonomous science', separable from the rest of physics, with its own irreducible laws and its own abstract nonphysical subject matter?

Presumably not. What it means, concludes the objection, is that *reductions are domain-specific*:

temperature-in-a-gas = the mean kinetic energy of the gas's molecules,

whereas

temperature-in-a-vacuum = the blackbody distribution of the vacuum's transient radiation.

Similarly, perhaps

joy-in-a-human = resonances in the lateral hypothalamus,

whereas

joy-in-a-Martian = something else entirely.

This means that we may expect some type/type reductions of mental states to physical states after all, though they will be much narrower than was first suggested. Furthermore, it means that functionalist claims concerning the radical autonomy of psychology cannot be sustained. And last, it suggests that functionalism is not so profoundly different from the identity theory as was first made out.

As with the defense of functionalism outlined earlier, I leave the evaluation of this criticism to the reader. We shall have occasion for further discussion of functionalism in later chapters. At this point, let us turn to the final materialist theory of mind, for functionalism is not the only major reaction against the identity theory.

Suggested Readings

Putnam, Hilary, "Minds and Machines," in *Dimensions of Mind*, ed. Sidney Hook (New York: New York University Press, 1960).
Putnam, Hilary, "Robots: Machines or Artificially Created Life?" *Journal of Philosophy*, vol. LXI, no. 21 (1964).
Putnam, Hilary, "The Nature of Mental States," in *Materialism and the Mind-Body Problem*, ed. David Rosenthal (Englewood Cliffs, NJ: Prentice-Hall, 1971).
Fodor, Jerry, *Psychological Explanation* (New York: Random House, 1968).
Dennett, Daniel, *Brainstorms* (Montgomery, Vermont: Bradford, 1978; Cambridge, MA: MIT Press).

Concerning Difficulties with Functionalism

Block, Ned, "Troubles with Functionalism," in *Minnesota Studies in the Philosophy of Science*, vol. IX ed. C. W. Savage (Minneapolis: University of Minnesota Press, 1978). Reprinted in *Readings in Philosophy of Psychology*, ed. N. Block (Cambridge, MA: Harvard University Press, 1980).
Churchland, Paul and Patricia, "Functionalism, Qualia, and Intentionality," *Philosophical Topics*, vol. 12, no. 1 (1981). Reprinted in *Mind, Brain, and Function*, eds. J. Biro and R. Shahan (Norman, OK: University of Oklahoma Press, 1982).
Churchland, Paul, "Eliminative Materialism and the Propositional Attitudes," *Journal of Philosophy*, vol. LXXVIII, no. 2 (1981).
Shoemaker, Sidney, "The Inverted Spectrum," *Journal of Philosophy*, vol. LXXIX, no. 7 (1982).
Enc, Berent, "In Defense of the Identity Theory," *Journal of Philosophy*, vol. LXXX, no. 5 (1983).

5. Eliminative Materialism

The identity theory was called into doubt not because the prospects for a materialist account of our mental capacities were thought to be poor, but because it seemed unlikely that the arrival of an adequate materialist theory would bring with it the nice one-to-one match-ups, between the concepts of folk psychology and the concepts of theoretical neuroscience, that intertheoretic reduction requires. The reason for that doubt was the great variety of quite different physical systems that could instantiate the required functional organization. *Eliminative materialism* also doubts that the correct neuroscientific account of human capacities will produce a neat reduction of our common-sense framework, but here the doubts arise from a quite different source.

As the eliminative materialists see it, the one-to-one match-ups will not be found, and our common-sense psychological framework will not enjoy an intertheoretic reduction, *because our common-sense psychological framework is a false and radically misleading conception of the causes of human behavior and the nature of cognitive activity.* On this view, folk psychology is not just an incomplete representation of our inner natures; it is an outright *mis*representation of our internal states and activities. Consequently, we cannot expect a truly adequate neuroscientific account of our inner lives to provide theoretical categories that match up nicely with the categories of our common-sense framework. Accordingly, we must expect that the older framework will simply be eliminated, rather than be reduced, by a matured neuroscience.

Historical Parallels   As the identity theorist can point to historical cases of successful intertheoretic reduction, so the eliminative materialist can point to historical cases of the outright elimination of the ontology of an older theory in favor of the ontology of a new and superior theory. For most of the eighteenth and nineteenth centuries, learned people believed that heat was a subtle *fluid* held in bodies, much in the way water is held in a sponge. A fair body of moderately successful theory described the way this fluid substance—called "caloric"—flowed within a body, or from one body to another, and how it produced thermal expansion, melting, boiling, and so forth. But by the end of the last century it had become abundantly clear that heat was not a substance at all, but just the energy of motion of the trillions of jostling molecules that make up the heated body itself. The new theory—the "corpuscular/kinetic theory of matter and heat"—was much more successful than the old in explaining and predicting the thermal behavior of bodies. And since we were unable to *identify* caloric fluid with kinetic energy (according to the old theory, caloric is a material *substance*; according to the new theory, kinetic energy is a form of *motion*), it was finally agreed that there is *no such thing* as caloric. Caloric was simply eliminated from our accepted ontology.

A second example. It used to be thought that when a piece of wood burns, or a piece of metal rusts, a spiritlike substance called "phlogiston" was being released: briskly, in the former case, slowly in the latter. Once gone, that 'noble' substance left only a base pile of ash or rust. It later came to be appreciated that both processes involve, not the loss of something, but the *gaining* of a substance taken from the atmosphere: oxygen. Phlogiston emerged, not as an incomplete description of what was going on, but as a radical misdescription. Phlogiston was therefore not suitable for reduction to or identification with some notion from within the new oxygen chemistry, and it was simply eliminated from science.

Admittedly, both of these examples concern the elimination of something nonobservable, but our history also includes the elimination of certain widely accepted 'observables'. Before Copernicus' views became available, almost any human who ventured out at night could look up at *the starry sphere of the heavens*, and if he stayed for more than a few minutes he could also see that it *turned*, around an axis through Polaris. What the sphere was made of (crystal?) and what made it turn (the gods?) were theoretical questions that exercised us for over two millennia. But hardly anyone doubted the existence of what everyone could observe with their own eyes. In the end, however, we learned to reinterpret our visual experience of the night sky within a very different conceptual framework, and the turning sphere evaporated.

Witches provide another example. Psychosis is a fairly common affliction among humans, and in earlier centuries its victims were standardly seen as cases of demonic possession, as instances of Satan's spirit itself, glaring malevolently out at us from behind the victims' eyes. That witches exist was not a matter of any controversy. One would occasionally see them, in any city or hamlet, engaged in incoherent, paranoid, or even murderous behavior. But observable or not, we eventually decided that witches simply do not exist. We concluded that the concept of a witch is an element in a conceptual framework that misrepresents so badly the phenomena to which it was standardly applied that literal application of the notion should be permanently withdrawn. Modern theories of mental dysfunction led to the elimination of witches from our serious ontology.

The concepts of folk psychology—belief, desire, fear, sensation, pain, joy, and so on—await a similar fate, according to the view at issue. And when neuroscience has matured to the point where the poverty of our current conceptions is apparent to everyone, and the superiority of the new framework is established, we shall then be able to set about *re*conceiving our internal states and activities, within a truly adequate conceptual framework at last. Our explanations of one another's behavior will appeal to such things as our neuropharmacological states, the neural activity in specialized anatomical areas, and whatever other states are deemed relevant by the new theory. Our private introspection will also be transformed, and may be profoundly enhanced by reason of the more accurate and penetrating framework it will have to work with—just as the astronomer's perception of the night sky is much enhanced by the detailed knowledge of modern astronomical theory that he or she possesses.

The magnitude of the conceptual revolution here suggested should not be minimized: it would be enormous. And the benefits to humanity might be equally great. If each of us possessed an accurate neuroscientific understanding of (what we now conceive dimly as) the varieties and causes of mental illness, the factors involved in learning, the neural basis of emotions, intelligence, and socialization, then the sum total of human misery might be much reduced. The simple increase in mutual understanding that the new framework made possible could contribute substantially toward a more peaceful and humane society. Of course, there would be dangers as well: increased knowledge means increased power, and power can always be misused.

Arguments for Eliminative Materialism

The arguments for eliminative materialism are diffuse and less than decisive, but they are stronger than is widely supposed. The distinguishing feature of this position is its denial that a smooth intertheoretic reduction is to be expected—even a species-specific reduction—of the framework of folk psychology to the framework of a matured neuroscience. The reason for this denial is the eliminative materialist's conviction that folk psychology is a hopelessly primitive and deeply confused conception of our internal activities. But why this low opinion of our common-sense conceptions?

There are at least three reasons. First, the eliminative materialist will point to the widespread explanatory, predictive, and manipulative failures of folk psychology. So much of what is central and familiar to us remains a complete mystery from within folk psychology. We do not know what *sleep* is, or why we have to have it, despite spending a full third of our lives in that condition. (The answer, "For rest," is mistaken. Even if people are allowed to rest continuously, their need for sleep is undiminished. Apparently, sleep serves some deeper functions, but we do not yet know what they are.) We do not understand how *learning* transforms each of us from a gaping infant to a cunning adult, or how differences in *intelligence* are grounded. We have not the slightest idea how *memory* works, or how we manage to retrieve relevant bits of information instantly from the awesome mass we have stored. We do not know what *mental illness* is, nor how to cure it.

In sum, the most central things about us remain almost entirely mysterious from within folk psychology. And the defects noted cannot be blamed on inadequate time allowed for their correction, for folk psychology has enjoyed no significant changes or advances in well over 2,000 years, despite its manifest failures. Truly successful theories may be expected to reduce, but significantly unsuccessful theories merit no such expectation.

This argument from explanatory poverty has a further aspect. So long as one sticks to normal brains, the poverty of folk psychology is perhaps not strikingly evident. But as soon as one examines the many perplexing behavioral and cognitive deficits suffered by people with *damaged* brains, one's descriptive and explanatory resources start to claw the air (see, for example chapter 7.3, p. 143). As with other humble theories asked to operate successfully in unexplored extensions of their old domain (for example, Newtonian mechanics in the domain of velocities close to the velocity of light, and the classical gas law in the domain of high pressures or temperatures), the descriptive and explanatory inadequacies of folk psychology become starkly evident.

The second argument tries to draw an inductive lesson from our conceptual history. Our early folk theories of motion were profoundly confused, and were eventually displaced entirely by more sophisticated theories. Our early folk theories of the structure and activity of the heavens were wildly off the mark, and survive only as historical lessons in how wrong we can be. Our folk theories of the nature of fire, and the nature of life, were similarly cockeyed. And one could go on, since the vast majority of our past folk conceptions have been similarly exploded. All except folk psychology, which survives to this day and has only recently begun to feel pressure. But the phenomenon of conscious intelligence is surely a more complex and difficult phenomenon than any of those just listed. So far as accurate understanding is concerned, it would be a *miracle* if we had got *that* one right the very first time, when we fell down so badly on all the others. Folk psychology has survived for so very long, presumably, not because it is basically correct in its representations, but because the phenomena addressed are so surpassingly difficult that any useful handle on them, no matter how feeble, is unlikely to be displaced in a hurry.

A third argument attempts to find an a priori advantage for eliminative materialism over the identity theory and functionalism. It attempts to counter the common intuition that eliminative materialism is distantly possible, perhaps, but is much less probable than either the identity theory or functionalism. The focus again is on whether the concepts of folk psychology will find vindicating match-ups in a matured neuroscience. The eliminativist bets no; the other two bet yes. (Even the functionalist bets yes, but expects the match-ups to be only species-specific, or only person-specific. Functionalism, recall, denies the existence only of *universal* type/type identities.)

The eliminativist will point out that the requirements on a reduction are rather demanding. The new theory must entail a set of principles and embedded concepts that mirrors very closely the specific conceptual structure to be reduced. And the fact is, there are vastly many more ways of being an explanatorily successful neuroscience while *not* mirroring the structure of folk psychology, than there are ways of being an explanatorily successful neuroscience while also *mirroring* the very specific structure of folk psychology. Accordingly, the a priori probability of eliminative materialism is not lower, but substantially *higher* than that of either of its competitors. One's initial intuitions here are simply mistaken.

Granted, this initial a priori advantage could be reduced if there were a very strong presumption in favor of the truth of folk psychology—true theories are better bets to win reduction. But according to the first two arguments, the presumptions on this point should run in precisely the opposite direction.

Arguments against
Eliminative Materialism
The initial plausibility of this rather radical view is low for almost everyone, since it denies deeply entrenched assumptions. That is at best a question-begging complaint, of course, since those assumptions are precisely what is at issue. But the following line of thought does attempt to mount a real argument.

Eliminative materialism is false, runs the argument, because one's introspection reveals directly the existence of pains, beliefs, desires, fears, and so forth. Their existence is as obvious as anything could be.

The eliminative materialist will reply that this argument makes the same mistake that an ancient or medieval person would be making if he insisted that he could just see with his own eyes that the heavens form a turning sphere, or that witches exist. The fact is, all observation occurs within some system of concepts, and our observation judgments are only as good as the conceptual framework in which they are expressed. In all three cases—the starry sphere, witches, and the familiar mental states—precisely what is challenged is the integrity of the background conceptual frameworks in which the observation judgments are expressed. To insist on the validity of one's experiences, *traditionally interpreted*, is therefore to beg the very question at issue. For in all three cases, the question is whether we should *re*conceive the nature of some familiar observational domain.

A second criticism attempts to find an incoherence in the eliminative materialist's position. The bald statement of eliminative materialism is that the familiar mental states do not really exist. But that statement is meaningful, runs the argument, only if it is the expression of a certain *belief*, and an *intention* to communicate, and a *knowledge* of the language, and so forth. But if the statement is true, then no such mental states exist, and the statement is therefore a meaningless string of marks or noises, and cannot be true. Evidently, the assumption that eliminative materialism is true entails that it cannot be true.

The hole in this argument is the premise concerning the conditions necessary for a statement to be meaningful. It begs the question. If eliminative materialism is true, then meaningfulness must have some different source. To insist on the 'old' source is to insist on the validity of the very framework at issue. Again, an historical parallel may be helpful here. Consider the medieval theory that being biologically *alive* is a matter of being ensouled by an immaterial *vital spirit*. And consider the following response to someone who has expressed disbelief in that theory.

> My learned friend has stated that there is no such thing as vital spirit. But this statement is incoherent. For if it is true, then my friend does not have vital spirit, and must therefore be *dead*. But if he is dead, then his statement is just a string of noises, devoid of meaning or truth. Evidently, the assumption that antivitalism is true entails that it cannot be true!   Q.E.D.

This second argument is now a joke, but the first argument begs the question in exactly the same way.

A final criticism draws a much weaker conclusion, but makes a rather stronger case. Eliminative materialism, it has been said, is making mountains out of molehills. It exaggerates the defects in folk psychology, and underplays its real successes. Perhaps the arrival of a matured neuroscience will require the elimination of the occasional folk-psychological concept, continues the criticism, and a minor adjustment in certain folk-psychological principles may have to be endured. But the large-scale elimination forecast by the eliminative materialist is just an alarmist worry or a romantic enthusiasm.

Perhaps this complaint is correct. And perhaps it is merely complacent. Whichever, it does bring out the important point that we do not confront two simple and mutually exclusive possibilities here: pure reduction versus pure elimination. Rather, these are the end points of a smooth spectrum of possible outcomes, between which there are mixed cases of partial elimination and partial reduction. Only empirical research (see chapter 7) can tell us where on that spectrum our own case will fall. Perhaps we should speak here, more liberally, of "revisionary materialism", instead of concentrating on the more radical possibility of an across-the-board elimination. Perhaps we should. But it has been my aim in this section to make it at least intelligible to you that our collective conceptual destiny lies substantially toward the revolutionary end of the spectrum.

Suggested Readings

Feyerabend, Paul, "Comment: 'Mental Events and the Brain,' " *Journal of Philosophy*, vol. LX (1963). Reprinted in *The Mind/Brain Identity Theory*, ed. C. V. Borst (London: Macmillan, 1970).

Feyerabend, Paul, "Materialism and the Mind-Body Problem," *Review of Metaphysics*, vol. XVII (1963). Reprinted in *The Mind/Brain Identity Theory*, ed. C. V. Borst (London: Macmillan, 1970).

Rorty, Richard, "Mind-Body Identity, Privacy, and Categories," *Review of Metaphysics*, vol. XIX (1965). Reprinted in *Materialism and the Mind-Body Problem*, ed. D. M. Rosenthal (Englewood Cliffs, NJ: Prentice-Hall, 1971).

Rorty, Richard, "In Defense of Eliminative Materialism," *Review of Metaphysics*, vol. XXIV (1970). Reprinted in *Materialism and the Mind-Body Problem*, ed. D. M. Rosenthal (Englewood Cliffs, NJ: Prentice-Hall, 1971).

Churchland, Paul, "Eliminative Materialism and the Propositional Attitudes," *Journal of Philosophy*, vol. LXXVIII, no. 2 (1981).

Dennett, Daniel, "Why You Can't Make a Computer that Feels Pain," in *Brainstorms* (Montgomery, VT: Bradford, 1978; Cambridge, MA: MIT Press).

Churchland, Paul, "Some Reductive Strategies in Cognitive Neurobiology," *Mind*, vol. 95, no. 379 (1986).

Chapter 3
The Semantical Problem

Where do the terms of our common-sense psychological vocabulary get their meanings? This apparently innocent question is important for at least three reasons. Psychological terms form a crucial test case for theories of meaning in general. The semantical problem is closely bound up with the ontological problem, as we saw in the first chapter. And it is even more closely bound up with the epistemological problem, as we shall see in the next chapter.

In this chapter, we shall explore the cases for and against each of the three main theories currently at issue. The first says that the meaning of any common-sense psychological term (of most of them, anyway) derives from an act of *inner ostension*. A second insists that their meaning derives from *operational definitions*. And a third claims that the meaning of any such term derives from its place in a *network of laws* that constitute 'folk' psychology. Without further ado, let us address the first theory.

1. Definition by Inner Ostension

One way to introduce a term to someone's vocabulary—"horse", or "fire engine", for example—is just to show the person an item of the relevant type, and say something like, *"That* is a horse," or *"This* is a fire engine." These are instances of what is called *ostensive definition*. One expects the hearer to notice the relevant features in the situation presented, and to be able to reapply the term when a new situation also contains them.

Of course, both of the expressions cited could have been introduced in another way. One could just have said to the hearer, "A horse is a large, hoofed animal used for riding." Here one gives the meaning of the term by connecting it in specific ways with other terms in the hearer's vocabulary. Such term introductions range from the explicit and complete ("An isosceles triangle is a three-sided closed plane figure with at least two equal sides") to the partial and casual ("Energy is what makes our cars run and keeps our lights burning"). But not all terms get their meaning in this way, it is often said. Some terms can get their meaning only in the first way, by direct ostension. Terms like "red", "sweet", and "warm", for example. Their meaning is not a matter of the relations they bear to other terms; it is a matter of their being directly associated with a specific quality displayed by material objects. Thus speaks orthodox semantic theory and common sense alike.

What of the terms in our common-sense psychological vocabulary? When one thinks of terms like "pain", "itch", and "sensation of red", ostension seems the obvious source of meaning. How could one possibly know the meaning of any of these terms unless one had actually had a pain, or an itch, or a sensation of red? Prima facie, it seems one could not. Call this "the standard view".

While the standard view may be correct for a significant class of psychological terms, it is clearly not correct for all such terms, nor even for the majority. Many important types of mental states have no qualitative character at all, or none that is relevant to their type-identity. Consider the variety of different beliefs, for example: the belief that P, the belief that Q, the belief that R, and so on. We have here a potential infinity of importantly different states. One could not possibly master the meaning of each expression by learning, one by one, a qualitative character peculiar to each state. Nor does each have a distinct quale anyhow. And the same goes for the potential infinity of distinct thoughts that P, and desires that P, and fears that P, and for all of the other 'propositional attitudes' as well. These are perhaps the most central expressions in our common-sense framework, and they are distinguished by a role-playing element, the sentence P, not by some introspectible quale ($=$ 'phenomenological quality'). Their meaning must derive from some other source.

Clearly the standard view cannot be the whole story about the meaning of psychological predicates. Further, the standard view is suspect even in its most plausible cases. Among those mental states that are associated with qualia, not all types have a *uniform* quale. In fact, very few do, if any. Consider the term "pain", and think of the wide variety of substantially different sensations included under that term (think of a headache, a burn, a piercing noise, a blow to the kneecap, and so on). Granted, all of these qualia are similar in causing a reaction of dislike in the victim, but this is a *causal/relational* property common to all pains, not a shared quale. Even sensations-of-red show a wide variation through many shades and hues, bordering on brown, orange, pink, purple, or black at their several extremes. Granted, intrinsic similarities do something to unify this diffuse class, but it seems clear that the class of sensations-of-red is equally delimited by the fact that sensations-of-red typically result from viewing such standard examples as lips, strawberries, apples, and fire engines. That is, they are united by their shared causal/relational features. The idea of meaning being exhausted by a single, unambiguous quale seems to be a myth.

Are we certain that knowing the quale is even necessary to knowing the meaning? It has been argued that someone who has never been in pain (perhaps because of some fault in his nervous system) could still know the meaning of the word "pain" and use it conversation, explanation, and prediction, just as we use it in describing others. Granted, he would not know what pain *feels* like, but he could still know all of its causal/relational properties, and hence would know as well as we do what kind of state pain is. There would remain *something* he did not know, but it is not clear that the something is the meaning of the word "pain".

If the meaning of terms like "pain" and "sensation-of-red" really were exhausted by their association with an inner quale, then we would be hard pressed to avoid a *semantic solipsism*. (Solipsism is the thesis that all knowledge is impossible save for knowledge of one's immediate self.) Since each one of us can experience only one's *own* states of consciousness, it would then be impossible for anyone to tell whether or not one's own meaning for "pain" is the same as anyone else's. And surely it is an odd theory of meaning that entails that no one ever understands what anyone else means.

These doubts about the standard 'inner ostension' theory of meaning have prompted philosophers to explore other approaches. The first serious attempt to articulate and to defend an alternative theory was provided by the philosophical behaviorists, whom we met in the preceding chapter. These thinkers advanced a further argument against the standard view, which we shall now examine.

2. *Philosophical Behaviorism*

According to the behaviorists, the meaning of any mental term is fixed by the many relations it bears to certain other terms: terms for publicly observable circumstances and behaviors. In its clearest formulations, behaviorism pointed to purely dispositional terms like "soluble" and "brittle" as semantic analogues for mental terms, and it pointed to operational definitions as the structures whereby the meanings of mental terms could be made explicit. The details of this view were outlined in chapter 2.2, so I shall not repeat them here.

A major problem for behaviorism was the insignificant role it assigned to the qualia of our mental states. But we have just seen some good reasons for reestimating (downward) the importance standardly assigned to qualia. And one of the most influential philosophers in the behaviorist tradition, Ludwig Wittgenstein, had a further argument against the standard view: the *private language argument*.

Despite the consequence of semantic solipsism, many defenders of the standard view were prepared to live with the idea that one's vocabulary for sensations was an inescapably *private* language. Wittgenstein attempted to show that a necessarily private language was completely impossible. The argument ran as follows. Suppose you attempt to give meaning to a term "W" solely by associating it with a certain sensation you feel at the time. At a later time, upon feeling a sensation, you may say, "There is another W." But how can you determine whether you have used the term correctly on this occasion? Perhaps you misremember the first sensation, or carelessly see a close similarity between the second and first where in fact there is only a faint and distant resemblance. If the term "W" enjoys no meaning connections whatsoever with *other* phenomena, such as certain standard causes and/or effects of the kind of sensation at issue, then there will be absolutely no way to distinguish between a correct use of "W" and an incorrect use of "W". But a term whose proper application is forever beyond determination is a meaningless term. A necessarily private language is therefore impossible.

This argument gave behaviorists much encouragement in their attempts to define our common expressions for mental states in terms of their connections with publicly observable circumstances and behaviors. Despite the encouragement, those attempts never really succeeded (as we saw in chapter 2.2), and frustration gathered quickly. Perhaps this should have been expected, because Wittgenstein's private language argument draws a stronger conclusion than its premises justify. If a check on correct application is what is required for meaningfulness, then all that one's understanding of "W" need include is some connections between the occurrence of the W-sensation and the occurrence of *other* phenomena. Those other phenomena *need* not be publicly observable phenomena: they can be other mental states, for example, and still serve as checks on the correct application of "W".

What Wittgenstein's argument should have concluded, therefore, is just that no term can be meaningful in the absence of systematic connections with other terms. Meaning, it appears, is something a term can enjoy only in the context of a network of other terms, terms connected to one another by means of general statements that contain them. If Wittgenstein and the behaviorists had drawn this slightly weaker conclusion, then perhaps philosophers might have arrived at the semantic theory of the following section more swiftly than they did.

Suggested Readings

Malcolm, Norman, "Wittgenstein's *Philosophical Investigations*," the *Philosophical Review*, vol. LXIII (1954). Reprinted in *The Philosophy of Mind*, ed. V. C. Chappell (Englewood Cliffs, NJ: Prentice-Hall, 1962).

Strawson, Sir Peter, "Persons," in *Minnesota Studies in the Philosophy of Science*, vol. II, eds. H. Feigl and M. Scriven (Minneapolis: University of Minnesota Press, 1958). Reprinted in *The Philosophy of Mind*, ed. V. C. Chappell (Englewood Cliffs, NJ: Prentice-Hall, 1962).

Hesse, Mary, "Is There an Independent Observation Language?" in *The Nature and Function of Scientific Theories*, ed. R. Colodny (Pittsburgh: Pittsburgh University Press, 1970). See especially pp. 44–45.

3. The Theoretical Network Thesis and Folk Psychology

The view to be explored in this section can be stated as follows. Our common-sense terms for mental states are the *theoretical terms* of a theoretical framework (folk psychology) embedded in our common-sense understanding, and the meanings of those terms are fixed in the same way as are the meanings of theoretical terms in general. Specifically, their meaning is fixed by the set of laws/principles/generalizations in which they figure. In order to explain this view, let me back up a few steps and talk about theories for a few moments.

The Semantics of   Consider large-scale theories, such
Theoretical Terms   as those found in the physical sciences: chemical theory, electromagnetic theory, atomic theory, thermodynamics, and so on. Typically, such a theory consists of a set of sentences—usually general sentences or *laws*. These laws express the relations that hold between the various properties/values/classes/entities whose existence is postulated by the theory. Such properties and entities are expressed or denoted by the set of *theoretical terms* peculiar to the theory in question.

Electromagnetic theory, for example, postulates the existence of electric charges, electric force fields, and magnetic force fields; and the laws of electromagnetic theory state how these things are related to one another and to various observable phenomena. To fully understand the expression "electric field" is to be familiar with the network of theoretical principles in which that expression appears. Collectively, they tell us what an electric field is and what it does.

This case is typical. Theoretical terms do not, in general, get their meanings from single, explicit definitions stating conditions necessary and sufficient for their application. They are implicitly defined by the network of principles that embed them. Such casual 'definitions' as one does find given (for example, "The *electron* is the unit of electricity") usually give only a small part of the term's significance, and are always subject to falsification in any case (for example, it now appears that the *quark* may be the unit of electricity, with a charge one-third that of the electron). Call this view the *network theory of meaning*.

The Deductive-Nomological   The laws of any theory do more,
Model of Explanation   however, than just give sense to the theoretical terms they contain. They also serve a predictive and an explanatory function, and this is their main value. Which raises the question: What is it to give an *explanation* of an event or state of affairs, and how do theories make this possible?

We may introduce the conventional wisdom on this point with the following story.

In my laboratory there is an apparatus consisting of a long metal bar with two facing mirrors, one attached to each end. The point of the bar is to keep the mirrors a precise distance apart. One morning, while remeasuring the distance just prior to performing some experiment, my assistant notices that the bar is now longer than it was, by about one millimeter.

"Hey," he announces, "this bar has expanded. Why is that?"
"Because I heated it," I explain.
"Y-e-s?" he queries, "what's that got to do with anything?"
"Well, the bar is made of copper," I explain further.
"Y-e-s?" he persists, "and what's that got to do with it?"
"Well, all copper expands when heated," I reply, suppressing exasperation.
"A-h-h, I see," he says, as the light finally dawns.

If, after my final remark, my assistant had still failed to understand, then I should have to fire him, because the explanation of why the bar expanded is now complete, and even a child should get it. We can see why, and in what sense, it is complete by looking at the assembled information my explanation contained.

1. All copper expands when heated.
2. This bar is copper.
3. This bar is heated.

----

4. This bar is expanded.

The reader will notice that, collectively, the first three propositions *deductively entail* the fourth proposition, the statement of the event or state of affairs to be explained. The bar's expansion is an inevitable consequence of the conditions described in the first three propositions.

We are looking here at a valid deductive *argument*. An explanation, it seems, has the form of an argument, an argument whose premises (the *explanans*) contain the explanatory information, and whose conclusion (the *explanandum*) describes the fact to be explained. Most important, the premises include a *nomological* statement—a law of nature, a general statement expressing the patterns to which nature adheres. The other premises express what are commonly called "initial conditions", and it is these that connect the law to the specific fact in need of explanation. In sum, to explain an event or state of affairs is to deduce its description from a law a nature. (Hence the name, "the deductive-nomological model of explanation".) The connection between comprehensive theories and explanatory power is now easy to see.

The *prediction* of events and states of affairs, we should note, follows essentially the same pattern. The difference is that the conclusions of the relevant arguments are in the future tense, rather than in the past or present tense. Notice also a further point. When voicing an explanation in ordinary life, one hardly ever states every premise of the relevant argument. (See my first response to my assistant.) There is generally no point, since one can assume that one's hearers already possess most of the relevant information. What one gives them is just the specific piece of information one presumes they are missing (for example, "I heated it"). Most explanations, as voiced, are only explanation sketches. The hearer is left to fill in what is left unsaid. Last, it should be pointed out that the 'laws' that lie behind our common-sense explanations are usually on the rough-and-ready side, expressing only a rough approximation to, or an incomplete grasp of, the true regularities involved. This is thus one further dimension in which our explanations are generally explanation sketches.

Folk Psychology   Consider now the considerable capacity that normal humans have for explaining and predicting the behavior of their fellow humans. We can even explain and predict the psychological states of other humans. We explain their behavior in terms of their beliefs and desires, and their pains, hopes, and fears. We explain their sadness in terms of their disappointment, their intentions in terms of their desires, and their beliefs in terms of their perceptions and inferences. How is it we are able to do all this?

If the account of explanation in the preceding section is correct, then each of us must possess a knowledge or a command of a rather substantial set of laws or general statements connecting the various mental states with (1) other mental states, with (2) external circumstances, and with (3) overt behaviors. Do we?

We can find out by pressing some common-sense explanations, as the explanation was pressed in the sample conversation earlier, to see what other elements are commonly left unsaid. When we do, argue the proponents of this view, we uncover literally hundreds and hundreds of common-sense generalizations concerning mental states, such as the following:

Persons tend to feel pain at points of recent bodily damage.

Persons denied fluids for some time tend to feel thirst.

Persons in pain tend to want to relieve that pain.

Persons who feel thirst tend to desire drinkable fluids.

Persons who are angry tend to be impatient.

Persons who feel a sudden sharp pain tend to wince.

Persons who are angry tend to frown.

Persons who want that *P*, and believe that *Q* would be sufficient to bring about *P*, and have no conflicting wants or preferred strategies, will try to bring it about that *Q*.

These familiar platitudes, and hundreds of others like them in which other mental terms are embedded, are what constitute our understanding of how we work. These rough-and-ready general statements or *laws* support explanations and predictions in the normal fashion. Collectively, they constitute a *theory*, a theory that postulates a range of internal states whose causal relations are described by the theory's laws. All of us learn that framework (at mother's knee, as we learn our language), and in so doing we acquire the common-sense conception of what conscious intelligence *is*. We may call that theoretical framework "folk psychology". It embodies the accumulated wisdom of thousands of generations' attempts to understand how we humans work.

To illustrate, briefly, the role that such laws play in ordinary explanations, consider the following exchange.

"Why did Michael wince slightly when he first sat down to the meeting?"
"Because he felt a sudden sharp pain."
"I see. And why did he feel a pain?"
"Because he sat on the tack I placed on his chair."

Here we have two explanations, one on the heels of the other. If each is pressed, in the manner of our initial example, the sixth and first laws on the preceding list will emerge from the presumptive background, and two deductive arguments will become apparent, showing the same pattern as the explanation of the expanded bar.

If folk psychology is literally a theory—albeit a very old theory, deeply entrenched in human language and culture—then the meanings of our psychological terms should indeed be fixed as the thesis of this section says they are: by the set of folk-psychological laws in which they figure. This view has a certain straightforward plausibility; after all, who will say that someone understands the meaning of the term "pain" if he has no idea that pain is caused by bodily damage, that people hate it, or that it causes distress, wincing, moaning, and avoidance behavior?

Qualia Again   But what of the qualia of our various psychological states? Can we really believe, as the network theory seems to require, that qualia play *no* role in the meanings of our psychological terms? The intuition that they do is extremely strong. There are at least two ways in which a defender of the network theory might try to handle this perennial intuition.

The first is just to admit that qualia do play *some* role in the meaning of *some* terms, though only a minor or secondary role at best. This concession would go a long way toward soothing our intuitions, and it is tempting just to adopt it and to declare the issue closed. But it does leave certain problems unsolved. Since the qualia of your sensations are apparent only to you, and mine only to me, *part* of the meaning of our sensation-terms will remain private, and it will still be a stubbornly open question whether any of us means the same thing by those terms.

The second compromise concedes to qualia a significant role in the introspective *application* of sensation-terms, but still attempts to deny that their role enjoys any *semantic* significance. The idea is that your introspective discrimination of a pain from a tickle, or a sensation-of-red from a sensation-of-green, is of course keyed to the qualitative character, in you, of the relevant states. Each of us learns to exploit such qualia as our states display, in order to make spontaneous observation judgments as to which states we are in. But what is strictly meant by "pain", for example, does not include any commitment to any specific qualia. The qualitative character of pains varies substantially even within a given individual; it may well vary even more widely across different individuals; and almost certainly it varies substantially across distinct biological species. Qualia, therefore, have an epistemological significance, but they are without semantic significance for terms in an intersubjective language.

Thus two competing addenda to the network theory of meaning. Which one should be adopted I leave to the reader to decide. In either case, the background lesson appears plain: the dominant, and perhaps the only, source of meaning for psychological terms is the common-sense theoretical network in which they are embedded. As with theoretical terms generally, one comes to understand them only as one learns to use the predictive and explanatory generalizations in which they figure.

General Significance   The significance of this network theory of meaning—for the mind-body problem—is as follows. The network theory is strictly consistent with all three of the current materialist positions, and it is also consistent with dualism. It does not by itself entail or rule out any of these positions. What it does do is tell us something about the nature of the conflict between them all, and about the way in which the conflict will be resolved. The lesson is as follows.

If our common-sense framework for psychological states is literally a *theory*, then the question of the relation of mental states to brain states becomes a question of how an old theory (folk psychology) is going to be related to a new theory (matured neuroscience) which threatens in some way to displace it. The four major positions on the mind-body issue emerge as four different anticipations of how that theoretical conflict is going to be resolved. The identity theorist expects that the old theory will be smoothly reduced by a matured neuroscience. The dualist maintains that the old theory will not be reduced by a matured neuroscience, on the grounds that human behavior has non-physical sources. The functionalist also expects that the old theory will not be reduced, but because (ironically) too many different kinds of physical systems can produce the exact causal organization specified by the old theory. And the eliminative materialist also expects that the old theory will fail to reduce, on the yet different grounds that it is simply too confused and inaccurate to win survival through intertheoretic reduction.

What is at issue here is the fate of a theory, the fate of a speculative explanatory framework, namely, our own beloved folk psychology. And it is apparent that the issue between these four possible fates is basically an empirical issue, to be settled decisively only by continuing research in the neurosciences, cognitive psychology, and artificial intelligence. Some of the available research results have already been marshaled in chapter 2. More will be explored in the final three chapters. The conclusion of this chapter—that our familiar self-conception is and always has been a theoretical conception in its own right—places all of those results in a deeper perspective.

As we shall see, the network theory of meaning also has major consequences for the vexing epistemological problems explored in the next chapter. We shall turn to those problems after examining one final issue concerning meaning: the *intentionality* of many of our mental states.

Suggested Readings

Sellars, Wilfrid, "Empiricism and the Philosophy of Mind," in *Minnesota Studies in the Philosophy of Science*, vol. I, eds. H. Feigl and M. Scriven (Minneapolis: University of Minnesota Press, 1956). Reprinted in Wilfrid Sellars, *Science, Perception, and Reality* (New York: Routledge & Keegan Paul, 1963); see especially sections 45–63.

Fodor, Jerry, and Chihara, C., "Operationalism and Ordinary Language: A Critique of Wittgenstein," *American Philosophical Quarterly*, vol. 2, no. 4 (1965).

Churchland, Paul, *Scientific Realism and the Plasticity of Mind* (Cambridge: Cambridge University Press, 1979), section 12.

Hempel, Carl, and Oppenheim, Paul, "Studies in the Logic of Explanation," *Philosophy of Science*, vol. 15 (1948), part I. Reprinted in *Aspects of Scientific Explanation*, ed. Carl Hempel (New York: Collier-Macmillan, 1965).

Churchland, Paul, "The Logical Character of Action Explanations," *Philosophical Review*, vol. LXXIX, no. 2 (1970).

4. Intentionality and the Propositional Attitudes

We have so far been exploring the language we use to talk about our mental states, and exploring theories as to the source of its meaning. Let us now direct our attention to certain of those mental states themselves—to thoughts, and beliefs, and fears, for example—for each such state also has a 'meaning', a specific propositional 'content'. One has

the *thought* that [children are marvellous],

the *belief* that [humans have great potential], and

the *fear* that [civilization will suffer another Dark Age].

Such states are called *propositional attitudes*, because each expresses a distinct 'attitude' toward a specific proposition. In the technical vocabulary of philosophers, such states are said to display *intentionality*, in that they 'intend' something or 'point to' something beyond themselves: they 'intend', or point to, children, humans, and civilization. (A caution: this use of the term "intentionality" has nothing to do with the term "intentional" as meaning "done deliberately".)

Propositional attitudes are not rare. They dominate our folk-psychological vocabulary. Recall that one can suspect that P, hope that P, desire that P, hear that P, introspect that P, infer that P, suppose that P, guess that P, prefer that P to that Q, be disgusted that P, delighted that P, amazed that P, alarmed that P, and so on and so forth. Collectively, these states constitute the essence of conscious intelligence, as folk psychology conceives it.

The intentionality of these propositional attitudes has occasionally been cited as the crucial feature that distinguishes the mental from the merely physical, as something that no purely physical state can display. Part of this claim may be quite correct, in that the rational manipulation of propositional attitudes may indeed be the distinctive feature of conscious intelligence. But though intentionality has often been cited as the 'mark of the mental', it need not constitute a presumption in favor of any form of dualism. We have already seen, in chapter 2.3, how purely physical states such as brain states might possess propositional content, and hence display intentionality. Having content or meaning, it seems, is just a matter of playing a specific role in a complex inferential/computational economy. And there is no reason why the internal states of a brain, or even of a computer, could not play such a role.

If certain states of our brains do play such a role, and if our mental states are in some sense identical with those states (as functionalism and the identity theory both claim), then we have here not a refutation of materialism, but rather a plausible explanation of how it is that our propositional attitudes have propositional content in the first place.

And if they have a distinct meaning or propositional content, then of course they will have reference (or attempted reference) as well: they will have the 'pointing beyond' themselves that originally characterized intentionality.

There is an historical irony in the fact that the propositional attitudes have occasionally been cited by philosophers as that which marks off the mental as utterly different from the physical. The irony is that when we examine the logical structure of our folk conceptions here, we find not differences, but some very deep *similarities* between the structure of folk psychology and the structure of paradigmatically physical theories. Let us begin by comparing the elements of the following two lists.

Propositional attitudes	Numerical attitudes
. . . believes that P	. . . has a length$_m$ of n
. . . desires that P	. . . has a velocity$_{m/s}$ of n
. . . fears that P	. . . has a temperature$_K$ of n
. . . sees that P	. . . has a charge$_c$ of n
. . . suspects that P	. . . has a kinetic energy$_J$ of n
$\vdots$	$\vdots$

Where folk psychology displays *propositional* attitudes, mathematical physics displays *numerical* attitudes. An expression on the first list is completed by putting a term for a specific proposition in place of "P"; an expression on the second list is completed by putting a term for a specific number in place of "n". Only then does a determinate predicate result. This structural parallel yields further parallels. Just as the relations between numbers (for example, being twice as large as n) can also characterize the relations between numerical *attitudes* (for example, my weight is twice your weight); so do the relations between propositions (for example, logical inconsistency, entailment) also characterize the relations between propositional *attitudes* (for example, my belief is inconsistent with your belief). The respective kinds of attitudes 'inherit' the abstract properties had by their respective kinds of abstract objects.

These parallels underlie the most important parallel of all. Where the relation between certain kinds of propositional attitudes, or between certain kinds of numerical attitudes, holds universally, we can state *laws*, laws that exploit the abstract relations holding between the attitudes they relate. Many of the explanatory laws of folk psychology display precisely this pattern.

• If x fears that P, then x desires that not-P.

- If x hopes that P, and x discovers that P, then x is pleased that P.
- If x believes that P, and x believes that (if P, then Q), then, barring confusion, distraction, and so on, x will believe that Q.
- If x desires that P, and x believes that (if Q, then P), and x is able to bring it about that Q, then, barring conflicting desires or preferred strategies, x will bring it about that Q.[1]

Similarly, the laws of mathematical physics display a precisely parallel structure, only it is numerical relations that are being exploited, rather than logical relations.

- If x has a pressure of P, and x has a volume of V, and x has a mass of μ, then, barring very high pressure or density, x has a temperature of $PV/\mu R$.
- If x has a mass of M, and x suffers a net force of F, then x has an acceleration of F/M.

Examples like this can be multiplied into the thousands. As well, many of the expressions in the physical sciences contain a term for a *vector*, and the laws comprehending such 'vectorial attitudes' characteristically display or exploit the *algebraic/trigonometric* relations that hold between the vectors denoted by those terms. For example,

- If x has a momentum of $\mathbf{P}_x$ and y has a momentum of $\mathbf{P}_y$ and x and y are the only interacting bodies in an isolated system, then the vector sum of $\mathbf{P}_x$ and $\mathbf{P}_y$ is a constant over time.

What is taking place in such examples is the same in all cases. The abstract relations holding in the domain of certain abstract objects— numbers, or vectors, or propositions—are drawn upon to help us state the empirical regularities that hold between *real* states and objects, such as between temperatures and pressures, forces and accelerations, interacting momenta, . . . and between various types of mental states. The conceptual framework of folk psychology is exploiting an intellectual strategy that is standard in many of our conceptual endeavors. And just as a theory is neither essentially physical, nor essentially nonphysical, for exploiting numbers or vectors; neither is a theory essentially physical, nor essentially nonphysical, for exploiting prop-

---

1. Strictly, these sentences should all be universally quantified, and there are qualifications to be made about terms and connectives as well. But since this introductory book presupposes no formal logic, I shall ignore these subtleties. The issues receive proper discussion in the paper by Paul Churchland listed in the suggested readings at the end of this section.

ositions. It remains an empirical question whether the propositional attitudes are ultimately physical in nature. The mere fact that they are *propositional* attitudes (and hence display intentionality) entails nothing one way or the other.

There are two apparent lessons to be drawn from this brief discussion. The first is the idea that since meaning arises from an item's place in a network of assumptions, and from the resulting conceptual role that the item plays in the system's ongoing inferential economy, therefore our mental states can have the propositional contents they do because of nothing more than their intricate *relational* features. This would mean that there is no problem in assuming that physical states could have propositional content, since in principle they could easily enjoy the relevant relational features. This view is now fairly widespread among researchers in the field, but it is not the universal opinion, so the reader is invited to be cautious.

The second lesson concerns the very close structural analogies that obtain between the concepts and laws of folk psychology, and the concepts and laws of other theories. The emergence of these parallels coheres closely with the view, already suggested in the preceding section, that folk psychology is literally a theory. Some further encouragement for this view will emerge in the next chapter.

Suggested Readings

Brentano, Franz, "The Distinction between Mental and Physical Phenomena," in *Realism and the Background of Phenomenology*, ed. R. M. Chisholm (Glencoe, IL: Free Press, 1960).

Chisholm, Roderick, "Notes on the Logic of Believing," *Philosophy and Phenomenological Research*, vol. 24 (1963).

Churchland, Paul, "Eliminative Materialism and the Propositional Attitudes," *Journal of Philosophy*, vol. 78, no. 2 (1981), section I.

Churchland, Paul, *Scientific Realism and the Plasticity of Mind* (Cambridge: Cambridge University Press, 1979), section 14.

Field, Hartry, "Mental Representation," *Erkenntnis*, vol. 13, no. 1 (1978). Reprinted in *Readings in Philosophy of Psychology*, vol. II, ed. N. Block (Cambridge, MA: Harvard University Press, 1981).

Fodor, Jerry, "Propositional Attitudes," *Monist*, vol. 61, no. 4 (1978). Reprinted in *Readings in Philosophy of Psychology*, vol. II, ed. N. Block (Cambridge, MA: Harvard University Press, 1981).

Fodor, Jerry, "Methodological Solipsism Considered as a Research Strategy in Cognitive Psychology," *The Behavioral and Brain Sciences*, vol. 3 (1980).

Stich, Stephen C., *From Folk Psychology to Cognitive Science: The Case Against Belief* (Cambridge, MA: MIT Press/Bradford, 1983).

Against the Inferential-Network Theory of Meaning and Intentionality

Searle, John, "Minds, Brains, and Programs," *The Behavioral and Brain Sciences*, vol. III, no. 3 (1980).

Chapter 4

The Epistemological Problem

The epistemological problem has two halves, both of them concerned with how we come to have *knowledge* of the internal activities of conscious, intelligent minds. The first problem is called the *problem of other minds*: How does one determine whether something other than oneself—an alien creature, a sophisticated robot, a socially active computer, or even another human—is really a thinking, feeling, conscious being; rather than, for example, an unconscious automaton whose behavior arises from something other than genuine mental states? How can one tell? The second problem is called the *problem of self-consciousness*: How is it that any conscious being has an immediate and privileged knowledge of its own sensations, emotions, beliefs, desires, and so forth? How is this possible? And just how trustworthy is that knowledge? The solutions to these problems, I think it will emerge, are not independent. Let us explore the first problem first.

1. The Problem of Other Minds

It is of course by observing a creature's behavior, including its verbal behavior, that we judge it to be a conscious, thinking creature—to be 'another mind'. From bodily damage and moaning, we infer pain. From smiles and laughter, we infer joy. From the dodging of a snowball, we infer perception. From complex and appropriate manipulation of the environment, we infer desires, intentions, and beliefs. From these and other things, and above all from speech, we infer conscious intelligence in the creature at issue.

This much is obvious, but these remarks serve only to introduce our problem, not to solve it. The problem begins to emerge when we ask what *justifies* the sorts of inferences cited. To infer the (hidden) occurrence of certain kinds of mental states from the occurrence of certain kinds of behavior is to assume that appropriate general connections hold between them, connections presumably of the form, "If behavior of kind *B* is displayed by any creature, then usually a mental state of kind *S* is occurring." Such 'psychobehavioral generalizations' have the form of standard empirical generalizations, such as "If a sound like thunder occurs, then usually there is (or was) a lightning strike somewhere in the vicinity." Presumably their justification is parallel also: such general statements are justified by our past experience of a regular connection between the phenomena cited. Wherever and whenever we perceive lightning, we generally perceive (very loud) thunder also, and barring the machinery of war, nothing else produces exactly that sound.

But how can one be justified in believing that the relevant psychobehavioral generalizations are true of other creatures, *when all one can ever observe is one-half of the alleged connection: the creature's behavior?* The creature's mental states, if he happens to have any, are directly observable only by the creature himself. We cannot observe them. And so we cannot possibly gather the sort of empirical support needed. Apparently then, one cannot possibly be justified in believing in such psychobehavioral generalizations. Accordingly, one cannot be justified in drawing inferences from another creature's behavior, to his possession of mental states. Which is to say, one cannot be justified in believing that any creature other than oneself has mental states!

This conclusion is deeply implausible, but the skeptical problem is quite robust. Belief in other minds requires inferences from behavior; such inferences require generalizations about creatures in general; such generalizations can only be justified by experience of creatures in general; but experience of one's own case is all one can have. This is the classical problem of other minds.

The Argument from Analogy

There are three classical attempts at a solution to the problem of other minds, and perhaps the simplest of these is the *argument from analogy*. One can observe both halves of the psychobehavioral connections in exactly one case, it is argued: in one's own. And one can determine that the relevant generalizations are indeed true, at least of oneself. But other humans are, so far as I am able to observe, entirely similar to me. If the generalizations are true of me, then it is a reasonable inference, by analogy with my own case, that they are also true of other humans. Therefore, I do have some justification for accepting those generalizations after all, and I am therefore justified in drawing specific inferences about the mental states of specific creatures on the strength of them.

Our impulse to resist the skeptical conclusion of the problem of other minds is sufficiently great that we are likely to grasp at any solution that promises a way around it. There are serious difficulties with the argument from analogy, however, and we should be wary of accepting it. The first problem is that it represents one's knowledge of other minds as resting on an inductive generalization from exactly *one* case. This is absolutely the weakest possible instance of an inductive argument, comparable to inferring that all bears are white on the strength of observing a single bear (a polar bear). It may well be wondered whether our robust confidence in the existence of other minds can possibly be accounted for and exhausted by such a feeble argument. Surely, one wants to object, my belief that you are conscious is better founded than *that*.

And there are further problems. If one's knowledge of other minds is ultimately limited by what one can observe in one's own case, then it will not be possible for color-blind people justly to believe that other humans have visual sensations that are denied to them, nor possible for a deaf person justly to believe that others can hear, and so forth. One can reasonably ascribe to other minds, on this view, only what one finds in one's own mind. This entails, for example, that one could not possibly be justified in ascribing mental states to an alien creature, if its psychology were systematically different from one's own (as, after all, it is likely to be). Are one's reasonable hypotheses about the contents of other minds really limited in these parochial ways?

A third objection attempts to undercut the argument from analogy entirely, as an account of how we come to appreciate the psycho-behavioral connections at issue. If I am to distinguish between and clearly recognize the many varieties of mental states, thereafter to divine the connections they bear to my behavior, I must possess the concepts necessary for making such identifying judgments: I must grasp the meaning of the terms "pain", "grief", "fear", "desire", "belief", and so forth. But we have already seen from the preceding chapter that the meaning of those terms is given, largely or entirely, by a network of general assumpticns connecting them with terms for other mental states, external circumstances, and observable behavior. Simply to possess the relevant concepts, therefore, is *already* to be apprised of the general connections between mental states and behavior that the examination of one's own case was supposed to provide. One's understanding of our folk-psychological concepts, therefore, must derive from something more than just the uninformed examination of one's own stream of consciousness.

Collectively, these difficulties with the argument from analogy have provided a strong motive for seeking a different solution to the problem of other minds. One that does not create problems of the same order as the problem to be solved.

Behaviorism Again   The philosophical behaviorists were quick to press a different solution, one informed by the difficulties discovered in the argument from analogy. Specifically, they argued that if the generalizations connecting mental states with behavior cannot be suitably justified by empirical observation, then perhaps that is because those generalizations were not empirical generalizations to start with. Rather, it was suggested, those generalizations are true by sheer *definition*. They are operational definitions of the psychological terms they contain. As such, they stand in no need of empirical justification. And a creature that behaves, or is disposed to behave, in the appropriate ways *is by definition* conscious, sentient, and intelligent. (Typical behaviorists were not always this bold and forthright in their claims, but neither were they often this clear in what they claimed.)

Given the pressure to solve the other-minds problem, the impotence of the argument from analogy, and the appeal of the idea that the meaning of psychological terms was in some way bound up with psychobehavioral generalizations, one can appreciate why philosophers tried so hard to make some variant of this position work. But they failed. When we examine the generalizations of folk psychology, we find that they seldom if ever take the form of simple 'operational definitions' (recall the discussion of the term "soluble" in 2.2). Behaviorists were unable to state the necessary and sufficient *behavioral* conditions for the application of even a single psychological term. Neither do the generalizations of folk psychology appear to be true by definition. They seem rather to be rough empirical truths, both in their effect on our linguistic intuitions and in their explanatory and predictive functions in everyday commerce. This fact returns us to the problem of trying to *justify* the various psychobehavioral generalizations on which one's knowledge of other minds seems to depend.

Explanatory Hypotheses   The problem of other minds was
and Folk Psychology   first formulated at a time when our grasp of the nature of theoretical justification was still rather primitive. Until fairly recently almost everybody believed that a general law could be justified only by an inductive generalization from a suitable number of observed instances of the elements comprehended by the law. One sees a number of crows, notices that each of them is black, and one generalizes to "All crows are black". And so for any law. It was thought. This idea might have been adequate for laws connecting observable things and properties, but modern science is full of laws governing the behavior of *unobservable* things and properties. Think of atoms, and molecules, and genes, and

electromagnetic waves. Plainly, laws concerning unobservables must enjoy some other form of empirical justification, if they are to be justified at all.

This other form of justification is not far to seek. Theorists postulate unobservable entities, and specific laws governing them, because occasionally this produces a theory that allows us to construct predictions and explanations of observable phenomena hitherto unexplained. More specifically, if we assume certain hypotheses, and conjoin with them information about observable circumstances, we can often deduce statements concerning further observable phenomena, statements which, it subsequently turns out, are systematically *true*. To the degree that any theory displays such explanatory and predictive virtues, that theory becomes a beliefworthy hypothesis. It has what is commonly called "hypothetico-deductive" justification (or "H-D" justification, for short). In sum, a theory about unobservables can be beliefworthy if it allows us to explain and to predict some domain of observable phenomena better than any competing theory. This is in fact the standard mode of justification for theories in general.

Consider now the network of general principles—connecting mental states with one another, with bodily circumstances, and with behavior—that constitutes folk psychology. This 'theory' allows us to explain and to predict the behavior of human beings better than any other hypothesis currently available, and what better reason can there be for believing a set of general laws about unobservable states and properties? The laws of folk psychology are beliefworthy for the same reason that the laws of any theory are beliefworthy: their explanatory and predictive success. Note further that one's justification here need owe nothing at all to one's examination of one's own case. It is folk psychology's success with respect to the behavior of people in general that matters. Conceivably one's own case might even differ from that of others (recall the 'alien creature' objection to the argument from analogy). But this need not affect one's theoretical access to their internal states, however different they might be. One would simply use a different psychological theory to understand their behavior, a theory different from the one that comprehends one's own inner life and outer behavior.

Turning now from general laws to individuals, the hypothesis that a specific individual has conscious intelligence is also an explanatory hypothesis, on this view. And it is plausible to the degree that the individual's continuing behavior is best explained and predicted in terms of desires, beliefs, perceptions, emotions, and so on. Since that is, in fact, the best way to understand the behavior of most humans, one is therefore justified in believing that they are 'other minds'. And one will be similarly justified in ascribing psychological states to any other creatures or machines, so long as such ascriptions sustain the most successful explanations and predictions of their continuing behavior.

Thus the most recent solution to the problem of other minds. Its virtues are fairly straightforward, and it coheres nicely with our earlier solution to the semantical problem. Both problems seem to yield to the assumption that our common-sense conceptual framework for mental states has all the features of a theory. Not everyone has found this assumption plausible, however, its virtues notwithstanding. If you center your attention on your direct consciousness of your own mental states, the idea that they are 'theoretical entities' may seem a very strange suggestion. Whether and how that suggestion might make sense will be addressed in the next section.

Suggested Readings

Malcolm, Norman, "Knowledge of Other Minds," *Journal of Philosophy*, vol. LV (1958). Reprinted in *The Philosophy of Mind*, ed. V. C. Chappell (Englewood Cliffs, NJ: Prentice-Hall, 1962).

Strawson, Sir Peter, "Persons," in *Minnesota Studies in the Philosophy of Science*, vol. II eds. H. Feigl, M. Scriven, and G. Maxwell (Minneapolis: University of Minnesota Press, 1958). Reprinted in *The Philosophy of Mind*, ed. V. C. Chappell (Englewood Cliffs, NJ: Prentice-Hall, 1962).

Sellars, Wilfrid, "Empiricism and the Philosophy of Mind," in *Minnesota Studies in the Philosophy of Science*, vol. I, eds. H. Feigl and M. Scriven (Minneapolis: University of Minnesota Press, 1956). Reprinted in Wilfrid Sellars, *Science, Perception, and Reality* (London: Routledge & Keegan Paul, 1963), sections 45–63.

Churchland, Paul, *Scientific Realism and the Plasticity of Mind* (Cambridge: Cambridge University Press, 1979), section 12.

2. The Problem of Self-Consciousness

Upon first reflection, self-consciousness is likely to seem implacably mysterious and utterly unique. This is part of what makes it so fascinating. Upon deeper reflection, however, the veil of mystery begins to part just a little, and self-consciousness can be seen as one instance of a more general phenomenon.

To be self-conscious is to have, at a minimum, *knowledge* of oneself. But this is not all. Self-consciousness involves knowledge not just of one's physical states, but knowledge of one's *mental states* specifically. Additionally, self-consciousness involves the same kind of *continuously updated* knowledge that one enjoys in one's continuous perception of the external world. Self-consciousness, it seems, is a kind of continuous apprehension of an inner reality, the reality of one's mental states and activities.

Self-Consciousness: A Contemporary View   The point about apprehension is important: evidently it is not enough just to have mental states. One must discriminate one kind of state from another. One must recognize them for what they are. In sum, one must apprehend them within some conceptual framework or other that catalogs the various different types of mental states. Only then will recognitional *judgment* be possible ("I am angry", "I am elated", "I believe that *P*", and so on). This suggests that there are different degrees of self-consciousness, since presumably one's ability to discriminate subtly different types of mental states improves with practice and increasing experience, and since the conceptual framework within which explicit recognition is expressed grows in sophistication and comprehensiveness as one learns more and more about the intricacies of human nature. Accordingly, the self-awareness of a young child, though real, will be much narrower or coarser than that of a sensitive adult. What is simply a dislike of someone, for a child, may divide into a mixture of jealousy, fear, and moral disapproval of someone, in the case of an honest and self-perceptive adult.

This suggests further that self-consciousness may vary from person to person, depending on which areas of discrimination and conception have been most thoroughly mastered. A novelist or psychologist may have a running awareness of her emotional states that is far more penetrating than the rest of us enjoy; a logician may have a more detailed consciousness of the continuing evolution of his beliefs; a decision-theorist may have a superior awareness of the flux of her desires, intentions, and practical reasonings; a painter may have a keener recognition of the structure of his visual sensations; and so forth. Self-consciousness, evidently, has a very large *learned* component.

In these respects, one's introspective consciousness of oneself appears very similar to one's perceptual consciousness of the external world. The difference is that, in the former case, whatever mechanisms of discrimination are at work are keyed to internal circumstances instead of to external ones. The mechanisms themselves are presumably innate, but one must learn to use them: to make useful discriminations and to prompt insightful judgments. Learned perceptual skills are familiar in the case of external perception. A symphony conductor can hear the clarinets' contribution to what is a seamless sound to a child. An astronomer can recognize the planets, and nebulae, and red giants, among what are just specks in the night sky to others. A skilled chef can taste the rosemary and shallots within what is just a yummy taste to a hungry diner. And so forth. It is evident that perception, whether inner or outer, is substantially a learned skill. Most of that learning takes place in our early childhood, of course: what is perceptually obvious to us now was a subtle discrimination at eight months. But there is always room to learn more.

In summary, self-consciousness, on this view, is just a species of perception: *self-perception*. It is not perception of one's foot with one's eyes, for example, but is rather the perception of one's internal states with what we may call (largely in ignorance) one's faculty of introspection. Self-consciousness is thus no more (and no less) mysterious than perception generally. It is just directed internally rather than externally.

Nor is it at all surprising that cognitively advanced creatures should possess self-consciousness. What perception requires is no more than that one's faculty of judgment be in systematic causal contact with the domain to be perceived, in such a way that we can learn to make, on a continuing basis, spontaneous, noninferred, but appropriate judgments about that domain. Our faculty of judgment is in causal contact with the external world, through the various sensory modalities; but it is also in systematic causal contact with the rest of the internal domain of which it is a part. Who will express surprise that one kind of brain activity enjoys rich causal connections with other kinds of brain activity? But such connections carry information, and thus make 'informed' judgment possible. Self-consciousness, therefore, at some level or to some degree of penetration, is to be expected in almost any cognitively advanced creature.

This view coheres with an evolutionary view. Presumably humanity has struggled toward self-consciousness in two dimensions: in the neurophysiological evolution of our ability to make useful introspective discriminations, and in the social evolution of a conceptual framework to exploit that discriminative capacity in prompting explanatorily and predictively useful judgments. As well, each of us is the site of an evolutionary struggle towards self-apprehension during his or her lifetime, in which we learn to use and to refine the innate discriminative capacities, and to master the socially entrenched conceptual framework (folk psychology) necessary to exploit them.

The Traditional View   These remarks on self-consciousness may seem plausible enough, but a long tradition in the philosophy of mind takes a very different view of our introspective knowledge. Introspection, it has been argued, is fundamentally different from any form of external perception. Our perception of the external world is always mediated by sensations or impressions of some kind, and the external world is thus known only indirectly and problematically. With introspection, however, our knowledge is immediate and direct. One does not introspectively apprehend a sensation by way of a sensation of that sensation, or apprehend an impression by way of an impression of that impression. As a result, one cannot be the victim of a false impression (of an impression), or a misleading sensation (of a sensation). Therefore, once one is considering the states of one's own mind, the distinction between appearance and reality disappears entirely. The mind is transparent to itself, and things in the mind are, necessarily, exactly what they 'seem' to be. It does not make any sense to say, for example, "It seemed to me that I was in considerable pain, but I was mistaken." Accordingly, one's candid introspective judgments about one's own mental states— or about one's own *sensations*, anyway—are incorrigible and infallible: it is logically impossible that they be mistaken. The mind knows itself first, in a unique way, and far better than it can ever know the external world.

This extraordinary position must be taken seriously—at least temporarily—for several reasons. First, it is part and parcel of an old and influential theory of knowledge-in-general: orthodox empiricism. Second, the claim that one's knowledge of one's sensations is unmediated, by further 'sensations$_2$', does seem plausible. And any attempt to deny it would lead either to an infinite regress of 'sensations$_3$', 'sensations$_4$', and so on; or to some level of 'sensations$_n$', where one's knowledge of them *is* at last unmediated. Third, the proponent of this view has a powerful rhetorical question. "How *could* one possibly be mistaken about whether or not one is in *pain*? How is it even possible to be wrong about a thing like that?" As the reader will note, this question is not easy to answer.

Arguments against
the Traditional View
The view that the mind knows itself first, in a unique way, and far better than it can ever know the external world, has dominated Western thought for over three centuries. But if one adopts a thoroughly naturalistic and evolutionary perspective on the mind, the traditional view quickly acquires a sort of fairy-tale quality. After all, brains were selected for because brains conferred a reproductive advantage on the individuals that possessed them. And they conferred that advantage because they allowed the individuals to anticipate their environment, to distinguish food from nonfood, predators from non-predators, safety from peril, and mates from nonmates. In sum, a brain gave them knowledge and control of *the external world*. Brains have been the beneficiaries of natural selection precisely because of that feature. Evidently, what they know first and best is not themselves, but the environment in which they have to survive.

The capacity for *self*-knowledge could conceivably be selected for as the incidental concomitant of the capacity for knowledge generally, and it might be selected for specifically if it happened to enhance in some way the brain's capacity for external knowledge. But in either case it would be at best a secondary advantage, derivative upon the increase in one's knowledge and control of the external world. And in any case, there is no reason to assume that self-perception, to the extent that it did evolve, would be fundamentally different in kind from external perception; and no reason at all to assume that it would be infallible.

If the traditional view is basically implausible, let us examine the arguments set forth in its favor, and see whether they withstand scrutiny. Consider first the rhetorical question, "How could one possibly be mistaken about the identity of one's own sensations?" As an argument for the incorrigibility of our knowledge of our sensations, it has the form, "None of us can *think* of a way in which we could be mistaken in our judgments about our sensations; therefore there *is* no way in which we could be mistaken." But this commits an elementary fallacy: it is an argument from ignorance. There may well be ways in which error is possible, despite our ignorance of them. Indeed, perhaps we are unaware of them precisely because we understand so little about the hidden mechanisms of introspection. The rhetorical question, therefore, could safely be put aside, even if we could not answer it. But in fact we can. With a little effort, we can think of many ways in which errors of introspective judgment can and do occur, as we shall see presently.

Consider now the argument that the distinction between appearance and reality must collapse in the case of sensations, since our apprehension of them is not mediated by anything that might misrepresent them. This argument is good only if misrepresentation by an intermediary is the only way in which errors could occur. But it is not. Even if introspection is unmediated by second-order 'sensations$_2$', nothing guarantees that the introspective judgment, "I am in pain," will be caused only by the occurrence of pains. Perhaps other things as well can cause that judgment, at least in unusual circumstances, in which case the judgment would be false. Consider the occurrence of something rather *similar* to pain—a sudden sensation of extreme cold, for example—in a situation where one strongly *expects* to feel pain. Suppose you are a captured spy, being interrogated at length with the repeated help of a hot iron pressed briefly to your back. If, on the twentieth trial, an *ice cube* is covertly pressed against your back, your immediate reaction will differ little or none from your first nineteen reactions. You almost certainly would think, for a brief moment, that you were feeling pain.

The incorrigibilist may try to insist that sensation number twenty was a pain after all, despite its benign cause, on the grounds that, if you took it to be a pain, if you thought it felt painful to you, then it really was a pain. This interpretation sits poorly with the fact that one can recover from the kinds of misidentification just explored. One's initial screech of horror gives way to "Wait . . . wait . . . that's not the same feeling as before. What's going on back there??" If sensation number twenty really *was* a pain, why does one's judgment reverse itself a few seconds later?

A similar case: the taste-sensation of lime sherbet is only very slightly different from the taste-sensation of orange sherbet, and in blindfold tests people do surprisingly poorly at telling which sensation is which. An orange-expectant subject fed lime sherbet may confidently identify her taste-sensation as being of the kind normally produced by orange sherbet, only to retract the identification immediately upon being given a (blind) taste of the genuinely orange article. Here one *corrects* one's qualitative identification, in flat contradiction to the idea that mistakes are impossible. Mistakes of this kind are called *expectation effects*, and they are a standard phenomenon with perception generally. Evidently, they apply to introspection as well. The reality of expectation effects provides us with a recipe for producing almost any misidentification you like, whether of external things or of internal states.

Further, do we really know enough about the mechanisms of introspection to insist that nothing mediates the sensation and the judgment about it? Granted, there is no intermediary that we are *aware* of, but this means nothing, since on any view there must be much of the mind's operation that is below the level of introspective detection. Here then is another possible source of error. The distinction between appearance and reality may be hard to draw, in the case of sensations, only because we know so little about the ways in which things can and do go wrong.

Another way in which sensations can be misjudged emerges when we consider sensations with very short durations. Sensations can be artificially induced so as to have durations of arbitrary length. Not surprisingly, as the durations become shorter, reliable identifications (of their qualitative identity) become harder and harder to make, and mistakes become, not impossible, but inevitable. Which is to say, the agreement between what the subject says the sensation is, and what its mode of production indicates it should be, is near-perfect for long presentations, but falls off toward chance as the length of the presentations approaches zero. Such 'presentation effects' are also standard in perception generally. And if the subject is suitably drugged or exhausted, the reliability of his identifications falls off even more swiftly. This too is standard.

Memory effects must also be mentioned. Suppose a person who, perhaps because of some neural damage in youth, has not felt pain or any other tactile or visceral sensation for *fifty years*, or has been color-blind for the same period. Does anyone really suppose that, if the subject's neural deficit were suddenly repaired after such a long hiatus, he would instantly be able to discriminate and identify (= recognize which similarity-class is instanced) every one of his newly recovered sensations, and do it with infallible accuracy? The idea is not at all plausible. Similar effects could also be produced in the short term, with a drug that temporarily clouds one's memory of the various types of sensations. Failures of identification and outright misidentifications would then be wholly natural. And even in the normal case, are spontaneous, isolated, and unnoticed lapses of memory utterly impossible? How can the defender of the traditional view rule them out?

A more familiar sort of case also merits mention. Suppose you are dreaming that you have a splitting headache, or that you are in excruciating pain from being tortured. When you awaken suddenly, do you not realize, in a wave of relief, that you were *not really* the victim of a headache, or of excruciating pain, despite the conviction that attends every dream? The incorrigibility thesis is beginning to look highly implausible.

None of this should be surprising. The incorrigibility thesis might have been initially plausible in the case of sensations, but it is not remotely plausible for most other mental states like beliefs, desires, and emotions. We are notoriously bad, for example, at judging whether we are jealous, or vindictive; at judging our most basic desires; and at judging our own traits of character. Granted, infallibility has seldom been claimed for anything beyond sensations. But this restriction raises problems of its own. Why should infallibility attend sensations, but not emotions and desires? Knowledge of the latter seems no more 'mediated' than knowledge of the former.

Intriguingly, recent research in social psychology has shown that the explanations one offers for one's own behavior often have little or no origin in reliable introspection, despite one's sincere beliefs to that effect, but are instead spontaneously confabulated on the spot as *explanatory hypotheses* to fit the behavior and circumstances observed (see the paper by Nisbett and Wilson cited in the suggested readings at the end of this section). And they are often demonstrably wrong, since the 'introspective' reports given prove to be a function of wholly external features of the experimental situation, features under the control of the experimenters. On the view of these researchers, much of what passes for introspective reports is really the expression of one's spontaneous *theorizing* about one's reasons, motives, and perceptions, where the hypotheses produced are based on the same external evidence available to the public at large.

Consider a final argument against the incorrigibility thesis. Our introspective judgments are framed in the concepts of folk psychology, which framework we have already determined (in chapters 3.3, 3.4, and 4.1) to have the structure and status of an empirical theory. As with any such judgments, their integrity is only as good as the integrity of the empirical theory in which the relevant concepts are semantically embedded. Which is to say, if folk psychology should turn out to be a radically false theory, then its entire ontology would lose its claim to reality. And any judgment framed in its terms would have to be deemed false by reason of presupposing a false background theory. Since folk psychology is an empirical theory, it is always strictly possible that it might turn out to be radically false. Accordingly, it is always possible that any judgment framed in its terms be false. Therefore, our introspective judgments are not incorrigible. Not only might they be wrong occasionally, and one by one; they might *all* be cockeyed!

The Theory-Ladenness of All Perception

The strangeness of the idea that mental states are 'theoretical' can be reduced by the following reflections. All perceptual judgments, not just introspective ones, are 'theory-laden': all perception involves speculative interpretation. This, at least, is the claim of more recently developed versions of empiricism. The basic idea behind this claim can be expressed with the following very brief, but very general, argument: the *network argument*.

1. Any perceptual judgment involves the application of *concepts* (for example, *a* is *F*).

2. Any concept is a node in a *network* of contrasting concepts, and its meaning is fixed by its peculiar place within that network.

3. Any network of concepts is a speculative assumption or *theory*: minimally, as to the classes into which nature divides herself, and the major relations that hold between them.

Therefore,

4. Any perceptual judgment presupposes a theory.

According to this general view, the mind/brain is a furiously active theorizer from the word go. The perceptual world is largely an unintelligible confusion to a newborn infant, but its mind/brain sets about immediately to formulate a conceptual framework with which to apprehend, to explain, and to anticipate that world. Thus ensues a sequence of conceptual inventions, modifications, and revolutions that finally produces something approximating our common-sense conception of the world. The furious conceptual evolution undergone by every child in its first two years is probably never equaled throughout the remainder of its life.

The point of all this, for our purposes, is as follows. At life's opening, the mind/brain finds itself as confusing and unintelligible as it finds the external world. It must set about to learn the structure and activities of its inner states no less than it must set about to learn the structure and activities of the external world. With time, it does learn about itself, but through a process of conceptual development and learned discrimination that parallels exactly the process by which it apprehends the world outside of it. The traditional view, it would seem, is simply mistaken.

Suggested Readings

Armstrong, David, *A Materialist Theory of the Mind* (London: Routledge & Keegan Paul, 1968), chapter 6, sections IX, X; and chapter 15, section II.

Dennett, Daniel, "Toward a Cognitive Theory of Consciousness," in *Minnesota Studies in the Philosophy of Science*, vol. IX, ed. C. W. Savage (Minneapolis: University of Minnesota Press, 1978). Reprinted in Daniel Dennett, *Brainstorms* (Montgomery, VT: Bradford, 1978; Cambridge, MA: MIT Press).

Nisbett, Richard, and Wilson, Timothy, "Telling More Than We Can Know: Verbal Reports on Mental Processes," *Psychological Review*, vol. 84, no. 3 (1977).

Churchland, Patricia, "Consciousness: The Transmutation of a Concept," *Pacific Philosophical Quarterly*, vol. 64 (1983).

Churchland, Paul, *Scientific Realism and the Plasticity of Mind* (Cambridge: Cambridge

University Press, 1979), sections 13 and 16; on the theory-ladenness of perception in general, see chapter 2.

Nagel, Thomas, "What Is It Like to Be a Bat?" *Philosophical Review*, vol. LXXXIII (1974). Reprinted in *Readings in Philosophy of Psychology*, vol. I, ed. N. Block (Cambridge, MA: Harvard University Press, 1980).

Chapter 5
The Methodological Problem

It is plain that the familiar conceptual framework of folk psychology gives one a nontrivial understanding of many aspects of human mentality. Equally plain, however, are the many aspects of conscious intelligence it leaves largely in the dark: learning, memory, language use, intelligence differences, sleep, motor coordination, perception, madness, and so on. We understand so very little of what is there to be understood, and it is the job of science to throw back the enveloping shadows and reveal to us the inner nature and secret workings of the mind.

On this much, all parties can agree. There is major disagreement, however, on how any science of mind should proceed if it is to have the best chance of success. There is disagreement, that is, on the intellectual *methods* that should be employed. Here follows a brief description and discussion of the four most influential methodologies that have guided research into the mind in this century.

1. Idealism and Phenomenology

Here it is useful to back up a few steps and provide a little history. While de la Mettrie (see p. 99) was trying to reduce mind to matter, other thinkers were concerned to effect a reduction in precisely the opposite direction. Bishop George Berkeley (1685–1753) argued that material objects have no existence save as the 'objects' or 'contents' of the perceptual states of conscious minds. To put the point crudely, the material world is nothing but a coherent *dream*. If one holds that the material world is merely one's own dream, then one is a *subjective idealist*. If one holds, as Berkeley did, that the material world is God's dream, a dream in which we all share, then one is an *objective idealist*. In either case, the fundamental stuff of existence is mind, not matter. Hence the term "idealism".

This is a startling and intriguing hypothesis. We are asked to think of the 'objective' material world as being nothing more than the 'sensorium of God': the material world stands to God's mind in the same relation that your sensory experience stands to your own mind. We are all of us spectators, somehow, of God's dream: the physical universe. This hypothesis may seem to some a faintly mad dream in its own right, but we can at least imagine how serious evidence might support it. Suppose we could provide detailed *explanations* of the behavior and constitution of matter, explanations grounded in theoretical assumptions about the constitution of the mind (ours perhaps, or God's). Idealism would then start to look genuinely plausible.

In fact, no genuinely useful explanations of this sort have ever been provided, and so idealism remains comparatively implausible. Explanations in the other direction—of various mental phenomena in terms of physical phenomena—are far more substantial. We need think only of evolutionary theory, artificial intelligence, and the neurosciences to see the breadth of the advancing materialist front. (These will be examined in detail in chapters 6–8.)

There was a time, however, when such idealist explanations of the material world did seem available. Immanuel Kant (1724–1804) made a lasting impression on Western philosophy when he argued, in the *Critique of Pure Reason*, that the familiar human experience of the material world is in large measure *constructed* by the active human mind. As Kant saw it, the innate forms of human perception and the innate categories of human understanding impose an invariant order on the initial chaos of raw sensory input. All humans share an experience, therefore, of a highly specific empirical world. Kant tried to explain, in this way, why the laws of Euclidean geometry and Newtonian physics were necessarily true of the world-of-human-experience. He thought they were an inescapable consequence of the mind's own structuring activity.

Both Euclidean geometry and Newtonian physics have since turned out to be empirically false, which certainly undermines the specifics of Kant's story. But Kant's central idea—that the general forms and categories of our perceptual experience are imposed by an active, structuring mind—is an idea that survives. The material objects in our constructed experience may therefore be empirically real (= real for all human experience), but they need not be transcendentally real (= real from a possible God's point of view).

This demotion of matter, to the principal category in a world of appearance, is characteristic of much philosophy since Kant. However, Kant added a second element to the story, which changes it from a purely idealist script, and marks Kant as a most atypical idealist. According to Kant, the world of inner sense, the world of sensations and thoughts and emotions, is *also* a 'constructed world'. As with its access to the 'external' world, the mind's access to itself is equally mediated by its own structural and conceptual contributions. It has access to itself only through its own self-representations. Though empirically real, therefore, the mind need not be transcendentally real, any more than matter need be. For Kant, the transcendental nature of mind-in-itself is as opaque as the transcendental nature of matter-in-itself. And in general, he thought, things-as-they-are-in-themselves (independent of human perception and conceptualization) are forever unknowable by humans.

Subsequent philosophers have been more optimistic than Kant about the mind's ultimate prospects for self-understanding. Many suppose that, through scientific research, the mind can make conceptual *progress*: toward the goal of reconceiving the material world, and the mind, in conceptual terms that do correspond at last to the true nature of things-in-themselves. This is the hope of *scientific realism*, a philosophical view that lies behind most of our current psychological and neuro-scientific research. The *phenomenological* tradition, though also optimistic about self-understanding, takes an interestingly different view.

Phenomenology is the name of a philosophical tradition centered in continental Europe. With roots in Kantian philosophy, it is a tree with many branches, but its various advocates are all agreed that a true understanding of the nature of mind can be achieved only by methods that are radically different from those that guide science generally. The reasons for this strong position derive in part from the theory of knowledge (the epistemology) embraced by phenomenologists. They are keenly aware, as are almost all philosophers since the work of Kant, that the world-of-our-experience is in large measure a constructed world. Our innate forms of perception, our innate forms of understanding, and our learned conceptual frameworks collectively structure for us the familar, common-sense perceptual world: our *Lebenswelt*, or *life-world*.

Standard scientific activity, on their view, is just a continuation of certain of these 'constructive' activities of the mind. We construct ever more intricate and more deeply interpretive conceptions of the objective world, and make them answer to the perceptual facts of our *Lebenswelt* by way of prediction, explanation, and so on.

But, insist the phenomenologists, such a constructive procedure is not the way to achieve a true understanding of the *mind*, the *author* of all this constructive activity. Such a procedure simply takes the mind farther and farther away from the original 'pure' phenomena, and wraps it ever more tightly in intricacies of its own construction. The concepts of physical science can never be anything more than the mind's con-structed interpretation of the 'objective' world. To understand the *mind*, by contrast, what we need to do is make a one hundred and eighty degree turn, and adopt a procedure of analysis and disinterpretation of our experience. Such a methodology will retrace and reveal the mind's structuring activity, and thus lead us back toward the essential nature of the mind itself. It is possible for the mind to intuit its own essential nature, since, in contrast to its knowledge of the objective world, the mind has, or can aspire to have, direct and unmediated access to itself. Such a program of analytical and introspective research will produce a level of insight and understanding that is both superior to and independent of any possible understanding that might be produced by the essentially constructive and interpretive procedures of ordinary science.

Beyond sharing something like the above perspective, phenomenologists come in very different varieties. Georg Hegel (1770–1831), one of the earliest figures in the tradition, advanced a novel version of objective idealism. The journey of the spirit toward ultimate self-knowledge, he thought, is a journey toward the dissolution of the distinction between the subjective self and the objective world. The historical advance of human consciousness, individual and collective, is just the slow and scattered process by which the still groggy Absolute Mind (= God = the Universe) aspires to reach *self*-consciousness. Each individual human 'consciousness' is just one aspect of that grander Mind, and the contrast between oneself and others, and between oneself and the objective world, will eventually collapse as the Absolute Mind finally achieves full self-recognition. In the meantime, our *Lebenswelt* is better interpreted not as the Absolute Mind's peaceful *dream*, but rather as the content of Its struggling attempts at self-conscious awareness.

Hegel is not typical of the later tradition, however, and phenomenology has no essential commitment to an idealist ontology. Edmund Husserl (1859–1938) is the central figure in the modern tradition. Husserl pursued his phenomenological research within a roughly Cartesian framework, in which mind and matter are equally real, and his dominant concern was to understand the *intentionality* of our mental states (see chapter 3.4). The introspective retracing of the constructive activities of the mind, he argued, reveals the source of our mental 'contents', and leads one to a purified and indubitable awareness of an individual transcendental self, behind the empirical or phenomenal self. Here, he thought, one can explore the indubitable foundations of human experience, and of all of the objective empirical sciences.

This brief sketch does not do justice to what is a very rich tradition, and no tradition of its magnitude can be refuted in a paragraph. The reader will perceive, however, that what we called in the last chapter "the traditional view" concerning introspection is in some form or other an important part of the phenomenological tradition. The idea that one can have some suprascientific knowledge of the self, some special form of knowledge other than through the medium of constructive, objectifying conceptualization, is common throughout the tradition. That view goes against Kant's own conviction that one's introspective self-knowledge is just as inevitably an instance of objectifying 'construction' as is one's knowledge of the external world. And it goes against the modern psychological evidence that one's introspective judgments are on all fours with perceptual judgments generally, and provide knowledge that is in no way distinguished by any special status, purity, or authority.

If *all* knowledge is inevitably a matter of conceptual construction and speculative interpretation (recall the conclusion of chapter 4.2), then it would seem that the 'special access' to the 'essential nature' of the mind sought by the phenomenologists is but a dream, and that the standard methods of empirical science constitute the only hope the mind has of ever understanding itself. This need not preclude admitting introspective judgments as data for science, and thus need not preclude 'phenomenological research', but it will deny the results of such research any special or unique epistemological status.

Returning to 'the standard methods of empirical science' does not produce instant unanimity, however, for there are several competing conceptions of what those 'standard methods' are or should be, as the following sections will reveal.

Suggested Readings

Marx, Werner, *Hegel's Phenomenology of Spirit* (New York: Harper and Row, 1975).
Spiegelberg, Herbert, *The Phenomenological Movement*, vols. I, II (The Hague: Harper and Row, 1960), see especially the discussion of Edmund Husserl, vol. I, pp. 73–167.
Dreyfus, Hubert L., ed., *Husserl, Intentionality, and Cognitive Science* (Cambridge, MA: MIT Press/Bradford, 1982).
Smith, D. W., and McIntyre, R., *Husserl and Intentionality* (Boston: Reidel, 1982).
Piaget, Jean, *Insights and Illusions of Philosophy* (New York: World Publishing Co., 1971), chapter 3, "The False Ideal of a Suprascientific Knowledge."

2. Methodological Behaviorism

Methodological Behaviorism represents a very strong reaction against the dualistic and introspective approaches to psychology that preceded it. A child of the present century, it is also a self-conscious attempt to reconstruct the science of psychology along the lines of the enormously successful physical sciences, such as physics, chemistry, and biology. Over the past half-century, behaviorism has been the single most influential school of psychology in the English-speaking world. The last two decades have forced the reappraisal and the softening of some of its doctrines, but it remains a major influence.

Central Theses and Arguments   Its central principles are not difficult to understand. According to behaviorism, the first and most important obligation of the science of psychology is to *explain the behavior* of whatever creatures it addresses, humans included. By "behavior", the behaviorists mean the publicly observable, measurable, recordable activity of the subjects at issue: bodily movements, noises emitted, temperature changes, chemicals released, interactions with the environment, and so forth. Of the objective reality of these phenomena there is no doubt, it is felt, and psychology cannot go astray by taking aim at animal *behavior* as its primary explanatory target. This contrasts profoundly with earlier views, which took the elements and contents of internal *consciousness* as the proper explanatory target for psychology.

Of comparable importance to most behaviorists, however, was the *way* in which behavior was to be properly explained. Common-sense explanations that make appeal to 'mental states' are regarded as seriously defective in various ways. Such explanations appeal to a body of folklore that has no proper scientific basis, and that may consist largely of superstition and confusion, as with so many of our past conceptions. The familiar mentalistic notions are ill-defined and without clear objective criteria for their application, especially in the case of nonhuman animals; individual introspection does not provide a uniform or reliable ground for their application even in the case of humans; mentalistic explanations are generally constructed after-the-fact, and the principles invoked display very little predictive power; and such 'inward-looking' explanations hide from us the very extensive role of any organism's external environment in controlling its behavior.

Instead of appealing to mental states, behaviorists proposed to explain any organism's behavior in terms of its peculiar environmental circumstances. Or, in terms of the environment plus certain observable features of the organism. Or, failing that, also in terms of certain *unob-*

servable features of the organism—dispositions, and innate and conditioned reflexes—where those features meet a very strict condition: they must be such that their presence or absence could always be decisively determined by a behavioral test, as the solubility of a sugar cube is revealed by its actually dissolving (the behavior) when placed in water (the environmental circumstance). In sum, explanations in psychology are to be based entirely on notions that either are outright publicly observable, or are operationally defined in terms of notions that are so observable. (Review chapter 2.2 for the notion of an operational definition.)

Behaviorists are (or were) willing to restrict themselves to these resources, and to urge others to observe the same restrictions, because these restrictions were thought to be the unavoidable price of making psychology into a genuine science. Putting aside the ancient conceptual apparatus of common sense seemed a small price to pay in pursuit of such a worthy goal. If those mentalistic notions really do have integrity, it was thought, then the behaviorist methodology will eventually lead us back to them, or to suitably defined versions of them. And if they have no explanatory integrity, then rejecting them is no real loss.

Furthermore, an influential view in a related field gave incidental support to the behaviorists. A scientifically minded school of philosophy called "logical positivism" or "logical empiricism" held the view that the meaning of any theoretical term, in any science, ultimately derived from its definitional connections, however devious, to *observational* notions, which derive their meaning directly from sensory experience. Certain philosophers of science connected with this school claimed specifically that any meaningful theoretical term had to possess an *operational* definition in terms of observables. Behaviorism, therefore, seemed only to be following the rules that were said to govern legitimate science generally.

Criticisms of Behaviorism   In adopting a frankly skeptical attitude toward the ontology of mental states, and toward our familiar conception of the causes of human behavior, the behaviorists provoked a strongly negative reaction from a wide variety of moralists, clerics, novelists, and from other schools of philosophy and psychology. The principal complaint was that behaviorism tended to dehumanize humans by arbitrarily ruling out of scientific court the very feature that makes us special: a conscious mental life. To some extent, this is a question-begging complaint. Whether humans are 'special', and if we are, what features make us so, are themselves scientific questions requiring scientific answers. Perhaps we are mistaken in our common-sense beliefs as to whether and why we are special. (It would not be the first time: recall the universal conviction that humanity is placed at the center of the physical universe.) And it is no weighty criticism of behaviorism just stubbornly to repeat our culturally entrenched convictions.

Even so, it is now widely agreed that behaviorism went too far in its initial claims and restrictions, further than is necessary to secure scientific status for psychology. For one thing, the positivistic view that any meaningful theoretical term has to admit of an operational definition in terms of observables was quickly seen to be a mistake. Most terms in theoretical physics, for example, do enjoy at least some distant connections with observables, but not of the simple sort that would permit operational *definitions* in terms of those observables. Try giving such a definition for "*x* is a neutrino" or "*x* has an electron in its lowest orbital shell". Adequate conditionals connecting such terms to observables always turn out to require the use of many *other* theoretical terms, and hence the definition is not purely 'operational'. If a restriction in favor of operational definitions were to be followed, therefore, most of theoretical *physics* would have to be dismissed as meaningless pseudoscience!

Current views on meaning tend to reverse the positivist's view entirely: the meaning of any term, including observation terms, is fixed by its place in the network of beliefs in which it figures. (The network theory of meaning was discussed in chapter 3.3.) Our mentalistic vocabulary, therefore, cannot be ruled out of science on sheer abstract principle alone. It will have to be rejected, if at all, on grounds of its explanatory and predictive shortcomings relative to competing theories of human nature.

Nor does it seem scientifically reasonable to deny or simply to ignore the existence of internal phenomena, to which we have at least some introspective access, however confused, and which play at least some role, however misunderstood, in the causal origins of behavior. Insofar as behaviorism urged us to ignore such phenomena entirely, and to treat humans as 'black boxes' with reflexes unexplicated in terms of the box's internal structures and activities, it went too far. It was needlessly restrictive and guilty itself of an overreaction to earlier excesses.

With the justice of these criticisms admitted, most thinkers have been inclined simply to forget behaviorism. But this is not an appropriate reaction. Current versions and current defenders of behaviorism are prepared to concede the criticisms mentioned. But certain important elements of behaviorism survive and may yet prove to be right.

One of behaviorism's best-known advocates over the years, B. F. Skinner of Harvard University, has recently urged a version of behaviorism in which the reality of internal phenomena is asserted, as well as our introspective access to them, and in which internal phenomena are assigned a perfectly legitimate role in psychology. Despite these concessions, Skinner urges three important claims. First, what we are 'specting' when we introspect is just the physiological state of our own body and nervous system, not any 'nonphysical' reality. Second, introspection gives access to only a very tiny portion of our internal states and activities, and is confused and unreliable even there. And third, the states we discriminate in introspection, though correlated with our behavior, need not therefore be the actual causes of our behavior.

We might begin the job of isolating the real (internal) causes of our behavior by examining again the environmental factors that control our behavior, and then tracing the causal effects of those factors inward. The role of the *environment* in controlling behavior remains a central feature of this approach, and the rationale is not difficult to perceive. Currently living species all owe their survival to the fact that their instances, more reliably than others, responded appropriately to their environments. Human psychology, or that of any other species, is the result of a long evolutionary shaping of environmentally controlled behaviors—for example, "Eat whatever smells good," "Fight with (or flee from) whatever attacks," "Mate with whatever looks good," and so forth. Where else should psychology begin but with the systematic study of such controls?

As we are about to see, there *are* other interesting places for psychology to begin. But the behaviorist research program remains a live option, and it would be a mistake to dismiss its recent versions out of hand.

Suggested Readings

Skinner, B. F., *About Behaviorism* (New York: Random House, 1974).
Dennett, Daniel, "Skinner Skinned," in *Brainstorms* (Montgomery, VT: Bradford, 1978; Cambridge, MA: MIT Press).
Chomsky, Noam, "A Review of B. F. Skinner's *Verbal Behavior*," *Language*, vol. 35, no. 1 (1959). Reprinted in *Readings in Philosophy of Psychology*, vol. I, ed. N. Block (Cambridge, MA: Harvard University Press, 1980).

3. The Cognitive/Computational Approach

Within the broad framework of the functionalist conception of mind discussed in chapter 2.4, we find two closely related research programs aimed at solving the mystery of conscious intelligence: *cognitive psychology* and *artificial intelligence*. Both approaches contrast with the traditional forms of behaviorism, in that both feel free to postulate or ascribe an intricate system of internal states to intelligent creatures in order to account for their behavior. Standardly, the states postulated are, in some way or other, 'information-bearing' states, and their collective interactions are a function of the specific information they bear. Hence the general characterization, "the information-processing approach", or more simply, "the computational approach".

Compare the case of a pocket calculator. Its various input states represent specific numbers and arithmetical operations, and the internal activities that follow are determined by the computationally relevant features of those states. In the end, the output states bear systematic and rule-governed relations to those input states. The same is supposed to be true of organisms that display natural intelligence, save that their input states represent many more things than just numbers, and the 'computations' they execute are concerned with far more things than mere arithmetical relations. They are also concerned with logical relations, for example, and with spatial shapes, social relations, linguistic structures, color, motion, and so forth. (Examples will be explored in the next chapter.)

The aim of cognitive psychology is to account for the various activities that constitute intelligence—perception, memory, inference, deliberation, learning, language use, motor control, and so on—by postulating a system of internal states governed by a system of computational procedures, or an interactive set of such systems governed by a set of such procedures. The aim is to piece together an outline of the actual *functional* organization of the human nervous system, or of the nervous system of whatever creature is under study.

This is a tall order, given the extraordinary complexity of intelligent creatures, and a piecemeal approach is almost always adopted. A theorist might concentrate attention on perception, for example, or on language use, and then try to piece together a computational system that accounts for the specific activities of that faculty alone. Such piecemeal successes can then be collected, as they occur, to form a general account of the organism's intelligence.

In formulating and evaluating these computational hypotheses, three criteria are relevant. First, the computational system proposed must succeed in accounting for the inputs and outputs of the cognitive faculty under study. If the faculty is perception, for example, then the computational system proposed must account for the discriminations the creature actually makes, given the physical stimulation of its sense organs. If the faculty is language use, then the system must account for our discrimination of grammatical sentences from nonsense, and for our ability to produce grammatical sentences almost exclusively. Generally speaking, the system proposed must do what the creature at issue succeeds in doing, or what its selected faculty does.

The first criterion is important, but it is too coarse grained to be adequate on its own. The problem is that there are many different ways to skin any given cat. For any desired relation between inputs and outputs, there are infinitely many *different* computational procedures that will produce exactly that relation.

The point is easily illustrated with an elementary example. Suppose you have a small calculator-like device that behaves as follows. For any number n entered on its keyboard, it subsequently displays the number equal to $2n$. One way in which it may compute its answers is just to multiply the input by 2. A second way would be to multiply the input by 6 and then divide that answer by 3. A third way would be to divide the input by 10 and then multiply that answer by 20. And so on. Any of these computational procedures will produce the same 'overt behavior', so far as the doubling of arbitrary numbers is concerned. But the calculator is presumably using only one of them. How might we determine which?

Here enters the second criterion for evaluating computational hypotheses. Procedures that produce the 'same behavior' at one level of analysis may show subtle differences at a more fine-grained level of analysis. For example, the second two procedures each involve two distinct operations, where the original involves but one. Other things being equal then, therefore, one would expect the second two procedures to take longer to complete the calculation. Careful measurement of the times involved, therefore, might reveal which of two calculators was using the simpler procedure. Further, error patterns can also help us to discriminate between hypotheses. If each computational operation has a small but finite probability of error on each execution, then the second two procedures will make errors more often than the simpler procedure. A long test run, therefore, may help us discriminate one procedure from another. The specific nature of the errors made may also tell us a great deal about the procedures that produced them.

The third criterion for evaluating computational hypotheses is obvious, for artifacts and for biological organisms alike: the computational procedures proposed must be consistent with the physical capacities of the creature's circuitry or nervous system. An acceptable hypothesis must agree with the 'hardware' or 'wetware' that is actually executing the computational activity at issue.

This third criterion is usually very difficult to apply, save at a very superficial level, because the neural machinery that constitutes an advanced nervous system is so tiny in its elements, so intricate in its connections, and so vast in its extent. Unraveling the nervous system, as we shall see in chapter 7, is no casual matter. As a result, this third criterion exerts a weaker influence than the first two on much of the theorizing in cognitive psychology. And perhaps that is only to be expected: in the case of most cognitive functions, we do not yet have the problem of choosing between equally adequate computational hypotheses. We are still trying to construct even *one* hypothesis that is fully adequate to the activity at issue. Even so, the second and third criteria are what keep cognitive psychology an honest empirical science, a science concerned with the question of how natural intelligence is actually produced.

By contrast, the research program of *artificial* intelligence has typically dispensed with all but the first criterion. The aim of this program is simply to design computational systems capable of any and all of the intelligent behaviors observed in natural organisms. Whether the systems proposed use the *same* computational procedures used by any given natural organism has usually been of secondary interest at best.

There are some compelling reasons for pursuing this alternative approach to intelligence. For one thing, there is no reason to believe that the computational procedures used by natural organisms must be the best possible procedures to achieve the relevant ends. Our evolutionary history and our biological machinery almost certainly place significant and probably arbitrary constraints on the kinds of procedures we can use. Highspeed electronic computing machines, for example, are capable of executing routines that are impossible for our nervous systems. And in any case, it is argued, we need to study not just intelligence-on-the-hoof, but also the many dimensions of intelligence-in-general. Moreover, advances on this latter front will probably promote our understanding of purely natural intelligence.

The contrast between the two approaches is evident, but in practice it often tends to disappear. One way to test a hypothesis about the information-processing activities of a certain creature is to write a program to execute the relevant computations, run it on a computer, and compare the output behavior against the creature's behavior. Here the pursuit of cognitive psychology will look much like the pursuit of artificial intelligence. On the other hand, the artificial intelligence researcher need have no compunction about turning to the behavior and introspective reports of real creatures in order to inspire the invention of clever programs. Here the pursuit of artificial intelligence will look much like cognitive psychology.

Artificial intelligence gets a closer look in the next chapter. Let me close this section by discussing an objection to both of the research strategies outlined. It may have struck the reader that, on the computational approach, conscious intelligence does not emerge as having a single unifying essence, or a simple unique nature. Rather, intelligent creatures are represented as a loosely interconnected grab bag of highly various computational procedures, rather in the way a fellow student once characterized my first car as "a squadron of nuts and bolts flying in loose formation."

As it happens, that description of my car was accurate and the conception of intelligence advanced by the computational approach may be accurate as well. The slow accretion of semiisolated control systems does make evolutionary sense. Nervous systems evolved by bits and pieces, the occasional accidental addition being selected for because it happened to give an advantageous control over some aspect of the creature's behavior or internal operations. Long-term natural selection makes it likely that surviving creatures enjoy a smooth interaction with the environment, but the internal mechanisms that sustain that interaction may well be arbitrary, opportunistic, and jury-rigged. It is no criticism of the computational approach, therefore, that it may so represent them.

Suggested Readings

Dennett, Daniel, "Artificial Intelligence as Philosophy and as Psychology," in *Brainstorms* (Montgomery, VT: Bradford, 1978; Cambridge, MA: MIT Press).

Johnson-Laird, P. N., and Wason, P. C., *Thinking: Readings in Cognitive Science* (Cambridge: Cambridge University Press, 1977).

Anderson, J. R., *Cognitive Psychology and Its Implications* (San Francisco: Freeman, 1980).

Boden, Margaret, *Artificial Intelligence and Natural Man* (New York: Harvester Press, 1977).

Pylyshyn, Zenon, "Computation and Cognition," *The Behavioral and Brain Sciences*, vol. 3 (1980).

See also the suggested readings throughout chapter 6.

4. Methodological Materialism

The methodology described in the preceding section is commonly called "the top-down approach", because one starts with our current understanding of what intelligent creatures do, and then asks what sort of underlying operations could possibly produce or account for such cognitive activities. In sharp contrast, the methodology described in this section starts at the opposite end of the spectrum, and is called "the *bottom-up* approach". The basic idea is that cognitive activities are ultimately just activities of the nervous system; and if one wants to understand the activities of the nervous system, then the best way to gain that understanding is to examine the nervous system itself, to discover the structure and behavior of its tiniest elements, their interconnections and interactivity, their development over time, and their collective control of behavior.

It is this methodology that guides the several disciplines collected under the term *neuroscience*, and it is essentially the same spirit that bids one remove the back cover of an alarm clock and take it apart to see what makes it tick. This approach to intelligent behavior has a very long history. The ancient Greek Hippocrates was aware that brain degeneration destroyed sanity; and the Roman physician Galen had already discovered the existence of and the difference between the somatosensory nervous system (the set of fibers that conduct 'touch' information to the brain) and the motor nervous system (the set of fibers that radiate from the brain and spinal cord in control of the body's muscles). Dissection of dead animals had disclosed their existence, and Galen discovered that localized lesions or cuts in the two systems of living animals produced localized tactile 'blindness' in the former case and localized paralysis in the latter.

Systematic progress into the structure and workings of the nervous system had to wait until more recent centuries, since religious authorities frowned on or prohibited outright the postmortem dissection of the human body. Even so, the gross anatomy of the nervous system had become more or less understood by the late 1600s. This gave only limited insight into its functioning, however, and real progress into the microstructure and microactivity of the brain had to wait for the development of modern microscopic techniques, for the development of chemical and electrical theory, and for the development of modern electronic measuring and recording instruments. As a result, the most significant developments have occurred in the present century.

The neuronal architecture revealed by these methods is breathtaking in its intricacy. The functional atoms of the brain appear to be tiny impulse-processing cells called *neurons*, and there are roughly 10^{11}

(a one followed by 11 zeros: 100 billion) neurons in a single human brain. To gain a usable conception of this number, imagine a small two-story house filled from cellar to rafters with coarse sand. There are as many neurons in your brain as there are grains of sand in that house. More intriguing still, the average neuron enjoys, by way of tiny fibers extending from it called *dendrites* and *axons*, about 3,000 connections with other neurons, so the interconnectivity of the entire system is truly extraordinary: about 10^{14}, or 100 trillion, connections.

Such complexity defeats any ready understanding, and we have only just begun to unravel it. Ethical considerations preclude free experimentation on living humans, of course, but nature is unkind enough to perform her own experiments, and neurologists are presented with a steady stream of variously traumatized brains, the victims of chemical, physical, or degenerative abnormalities. Much can be learned from surgery, or from postmortem examinations, in such cases. Creatures with very simple nervous systems provide another route toward understanding. The nervous system of a sea slug, for example, contains only about 10,000 neurons, and that is a network that researchers have already mapped in its entirety. The chemical story of its habituation to certain stimuli—a primitive case of learning—has also been wrung from microexperimentation. The insights gained in such cases help us to address the neural activities of more complex creatures, such as lobsters, rats, monkeys—and humans.

The conviction of methodological materialism is that if we set about to understand the physical, chemical, electrical, and developmental behavior of neurons, and especially of systems of neurons, and the ways in which they exert control over one another and over behavior, then we will be on our way toward understanding everything there is to know about natural intelligence. It is true that the bottom-up approach does not address directly the familiar mentalistic phenomena recognized in folk psychology, but that fact can be seen as a virtue of the approach. If the thumb-worn categories of folk psychology (belief, desire, consciousness, and so on) really do possess objective integrity, then the bottom-up approach will eventually lead us back to them. And if they do not, then the bottom-up approach, being so closely tied to the empirical brain, offers the best hope for constructing a new and more adequate set of concepts with which to understand our inner life. Evidently, it is this methodology that gives the most direct expression to the philosophical themes advanced by the reductive and eliminative materialists.

It may be felt that such a ruthlessly materialistic approach degrades or seriously underestimates the true nature of conscious intelligence. But the materialist reply is that such a reaction itself degrades and seriously underestimates the power and virtuosity of the human *brain*, as it continues to reveal itself through neuroscientific research. What some of that research consists in, and how it throws light on questions concerning conscious intelligence, will be examined in chapter 7.

Suggested Readings

See the listings after each of the several sections in chapter 7.

Chapter 6
Artificial Intelligence

Is it possible to construct and configure a purely physical device so that it will possess genuine intelligence? The conviction of the research program called "artificial intelligence" ("AI", for short) is that it is possible, and the aim of this program is to realize that goal. What the program involves, and why its practitioners are optimistic, is the topic of this chapter. Some problems confronting the program will also be discussed.

Hopeful stabs in the direction of artificial intelligent behavior have a long history. In the second half of Descartes' century, the German mathematician and philosopher Gottfried Leibniz built a device that could add and subtract by means of interconnected rotating cylinders. He also argued for the possibility of a perfectly logical language in which all thinking would be reduced to sheer computation. He had no very clear idea of this language, but, as we shall see, the idea was prophetic.

In the century after Descartes, a physiological thinker named Julien de la Mettrie was similarly impressed by the mechanism of the human body, and by the idea that 'vital' activity arose not from a principle intrinsic to matter, nor from any nonmaterial substance, but from the physical structure and the resulting functional *organization* that matter could come to enjoy. But where Descartes shrank from the further conclusion this suggested, de la Mettrie plunged forward. Not only do our 'vital' activities result from the organization of physical matter, he declared, but so do all of our *mental* activities.

His book, *Man, a Machine*, was widely vilified, but once loosed, these ideas would not be stilled. De la Mettrie's contemporary, Jacques de Vaucanson, designed and constructed several very handsome and lifelike statues whose inner mechanical and pneumatic workings produced a variety of simple behaviors. A gilded copper duck put on a convincing display of drinking, eating, quacking, and splashing about in the water. And a life-sized human statue is alleged to have played a very credible flute. While these limited automata are unlikely to impress current opinion, no doubt their sudden activation gave a lasting jolt to the unsuspecting eighteenth-century observer.

More specifically *mental* capacities were addressed in the last century by the Cambridge mathematician Charles Babbage, whose carefully designed *Analytical Engine* was capable of all of the elementary logical and arithmetical operations, and whose principles foreshadowed the modern digital computer. Babbage was still limited to purely mechanical devices, however, and though his detailed design would certainly have worked had it been physically realized, a working machine was never undertaken because of its great mechanical complexity.

The complexity involved in all intelligent activity formed a continuing barrier to its easy simulation by mechanical devices, a barrier that has taken, since Babbage, a century for technology to surmount. The intervening time was not wasted, however. Fundamental progress was made in the abstract domain: in our understanding of the logic of propositions, the logic of classes, and the logical structure of geometry, arithmetic, and algebra. We came to appreciate the abstract notion of a *formal system*, of which the systems listed are all examples. A formal system consists of (1) a set of *formulae*, and (2) a set of *transformation rules* for manipulating them. The formulae are formed by joining, according to specified formation rules, several items from a basic store of *elements*. The transformation rules are concerned with the *formal structure* of any given formula (= the pattern in which its elements are combined), and their function is just to transform one formula into another formula.

In the case of elementary algebra, the basic elements are the numerals from 0 to 9, variables "a", "b", "c", ..., "(", ")", "=", "+", "−", "/", and "×". The formulae are terms, such as "$(12 - 4)/2$", or equations, such as "$x = (12 - 4)/2$". A sequence of transformations might be

$$x = (12 - 4)/2$$

$$x = 8/2$$

$$x = 4$$

These transformation rules you know, as well as what can be done with them. So you already possess a self-conscious command of at least one formal system. And given that you can think at all, you also have at least some tacit command of the general logic of propositions as well, which is another formal system.

There are endless possible formal systems, most of them trivial and uninteresting. But many of them are extraordinarily powerful, as the examples of logic and mathematics will attest. What is more interesting, from the point of view of AI, is that any formal system can, in principle, be automated. That is, the elements and operations of any formal system are always of a kind that a suitably constructed physical device *could* formulate and manipulate on its own. The actual construction of a suitable device, of course, may be unfeasible for reasons of scale or time or technology. But in the second half of the present century, developments in electronics made possible the construction of the high-speed, general-purpose digital computer. Such machines have made possible the automation of very powerful formal systems, and they are correspondingly capable of very powerful forms of computation. The barrier that frustrated Babbage has been shattered.

1. Computers: Some Elementary Concepts

Hardware   The term "hardware" refers to the physical computer itself and its peripheral devices, such as the keyboard for input, video screens and printers for outputs, and external or 'passive' memory tapes/disks/ drums for both (figure 6.1). It contrasts with the term "software", which denotes a sequence of instructions that tell the hardware what to do.

The computer proper consists of two main elements: the *central processing unit* (CPU), and the *active memory*, which is generally of the random access (RAM) type. This last expression means that the information-storing elements of the memory are arranged on an electronic grid, so that each element or 'register' enjoys a unique 'address' accessible directly by the central processing unit. This allows the CPU to find out what is in any given register straightaway, without searching laboriously through the entire sequence of many thousands of such

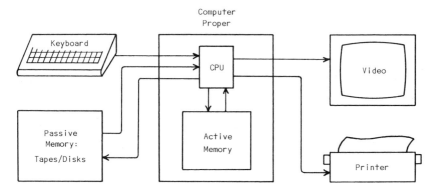

Figure 6.1

registers to find something needed. Correlatively, the CPU can also put information into a specific register straightaway. It has free and direct access to any element of an active memory of this type. Hence, "random access memory" or "RAM". The active memory serves as a 'scratch pad' or 'work space' for the CPU, and it also holds the instructions or *program* that we put in to tell the CPU specifically what to do.

The central processing unit is the functional core of the system. It is the manipulator of the various formulae fed into it; it embodies and executes the basic transformation rules of the machine. Computation, or information processing, consists in the rule-governed transformation of formulae into other formulae, and that is the job of the CPU.

Just what formulae does the CPU handle, and how does it transform them? The formal system that the standard computer is built to manipulate is exceedingly austere. It has only *two* basic elements—we may call them "1" and "0"—from which *all* of its formulae must be constructed. This is called the *machine code* or the *machine language*, and any formula in it is a finite string of 1's and 0's. These are represented in the machine itself as a charged or uncharged state of each element of the active memory, and as a pulse or no-pulse in the various pathways of the CPU.

Constructed or 'hard-wired' into the CPU are a large number of tiny elements called *logic gates*, which take a 1 or a 0 at each input port, and give a 1 or a 0 as output, where the output given is strictly determined by the nature of the gate and the elements of the input. By using entire banks of logic gates, entire strings of 1's and 0's can be transformed into new strings of differently ordered 1's and 0's, depending on how and where they are fed into the CPU. Here is where the *rule-governed transformations* occur.

What is intriguing about this tedious manipulation of formulae—aside from the astonishing speed with which it is done: over a million transformations per second—is that certain of the strings can be systematically *interpreted* as representing ordinary *numbers*, and certain subunits of the CPU can be interpreted as adders, multipliers, dividers, and so on. Any number can be expressed in *binary code*, rather than in our familiar decimal code. They can be expressed, that is, as strings of 1's and 0's.[1] And when they are, the input strings S_1 and S_2, and

1. In decimal notation, the columns, starting from the right, go from 0 up to 9, and if a number is larger than the rightmost column can represent, we spill over to the next column, which goes from 0 to 9, denoting tens this time. And so forth. In binary notation, the rightmost column goes only from 0 to 1, and *then* spills over to the next column, which also goes from 0 to 1, denoting twos this time. It spills over into the third column, denoting fours. And so on. For example, in binary notation, the familiar "1 + 2 = 3" becomes "1 + 10 = 11"; and "4 + 5 = 9" becomes "100 + 101 = 1001".

output string S_3, of a certain subunit of the CPU are always related so that, considered as numbers and not just as uninterpreted strings, S_3 always equals $S_1 + S_2$. That subunit—a set of logic gates, suitably connected—functions as an *adder*. Other subunits perform the other basic arithmetic functions.

Similarly, we can use machine language to encode formulae from propositional logic (these represent sentences in natural language), and certain subunits of the CPU will process those strings so that the output string always represents another formula, one which is the logical *conjunction* of those represented by the input strings, or their *disjunction*, or *negation*, or *conditionalization*. Equally, input strings representing arbitrary statements ("if-then" statements, for example) can be processed so that the output string represents a verdict concerning the truth-functional validity of the original statement.

CPUs are constructed with a command of all of the most basic logical and arithmetical operations, and endlessly many more operations can be managed by combining the elementary ones into more complex ones, and by combining these in turn, as is done when we write programs. Evidently, this boring manipulation of strings of 1's and 0's can amount to some very exciting forms of computational activity, powerful in depth and complexity, as well as in speed.

Software   The computational activity of the CPU can be controlled, and the term "software" refers to the sequence of instructions or *program* that exercises such control. A program is loaded into the computer's active memory, where its individual instructions are read and executed in sequence by the CPU. The program tells the CPU which input strings to process and in what ways, where and when to store the results in memory, when to retrieve them, display them, print them out, and so forth.

Accordingly, a specific program converts the computer into a 'special-purpose' machine. And given that there are a potentially infinite number of distinct programs, we can make the computer behave like a potentially infinite number of distinct 'special-purpose' machines. This is one of the reasons why the computers here described are called "general-purpose" machines. And there is a deeper reason, which we shall see presently.

At the most basic level, a program of instructions must be fed into the CPU in machine language, as strings of 1's and 0's, for that is the only language the CPU understands ($=$ is the only formal system the CPU is built to manipulate). But machine language is a most awkward and opaque language for humans to deal with. The strings that represent specific numbers, equations, and propositions, and the strings that represent instructions to perform logical and arithmetical operations look the same, to all but the most sophisticated programmer, as strings that represent nothing at all: a uniform gibberish of 1's and 0's. Clearly it would be better if we could translate machine language into a language more accessible to humans.

This can indeed be done, and since a translation is one case of a transformation of one kind of formula into another kind, and since a computer is a transformation device par excellence, we can even make *it* do the work for us. The first step is to construct the input keyboard so that each of the familiar characters, when hit, is sent to the computer proper coded as a unique eight-unit string of 1's and 0's. This preliminary coding is usually an instance of the ASCII code (American Standard Code for Information Interchange). Sequences of characters, such as "ADD 7, 5", can thus at least be represented in the vocabulary of the machine language. The next step is to load the computer with a program (laboriously written in machine language, but the job need be done only once) to *tra 1sform* these strings into strings of the machine language that, for example, really instruct the CPU to add the binary equivalent of 7 to the binary equivalent of 5. The same program can transform the resulting output (1100) back into ASCII code (00110001, 00110010), and the ASCII-coded printer, upon receipt of same, will print out the sequence of familiar numbers or letters desired, in this case, "12".

Such a program is called an *interpreter*, or a *compiler*, or an *assembler*, and the reader will perceive that this strategy can achieve not only a more 'friendly' interaction between human and machine, but major economies of expression as well. A single expression such as "AVERAGE $X_1, X_2, \ldots, X_n$" can be transformed (first into ASCII code, and then) into a long machine-language string that combines a number of distinct basic operations like adding and dividing. One instruction in the higher-level language then produces the execution of a great many instructions in the machine language. Such higher-level languages are called *programming languages*, and they are as close as most programmers ever get to the austere notation of the machine language.

It is evident that, once loaded with an interpreter to permit the use of a high-level programming language, the computer is now manipulating the formulae of a new formal system, some of whose 'basic' transformations are more sophisticated than those displayed in the formal system of the machine language. Our original computer is now *simulating* a different computer, one built to manipulate strings in the *programming* language. As far as the person using this 'new' computer is concerned, the 'new' language *is* the computer's language. For this reason, the computer-plus-interpreter is often called "the virtual machine".

All of this means that one information-processing system, differently programmed, can simulate many quite different information-processing systems. Which suggests that a computer, suitably programmed, might be able to simulate the information-processing systems found in the nervous systems of biological creatures. Certain results in abstract computing theory lend strong support to this expectation. If a given computer meets certain functional conditions, then it is an instance of what theorists call a *universal Turing machine* (named after the pioneer computer theorist Alan M. Turing). The interesting thing about a universal Turing machine is that, *for any well-defined computational procedures whatever, a universal Turing machine is capable of simulating a machine that will execute those procedures.* It does this by reproducing exactly the input/output behavior of the machine being simulated. And the exciting fact is, the modern computer *is* a universal Turing machine. (One qualification: real computers lack unlimited memories. But memory can always be made larger to meet demand.) This is the deeper sense, alluded to earlier, in which modern digital computers are 'general-purpose' machines.

The question that confronts the research program of AI, therefore, is not whether suitably programmed computers can simulate the continuing behavior produced by the computational procedures found in natural animals, including those found in humans. That question is generally regarded as settled. In principle, at least, they can. The important question is whether the activities that constitute conscious intelligence are all *computational procedures* of some kind or other. The guiding assumption of AI is that they are, and its aim is to construct actual programs that will simulate them.

That is why the vast majority of AI workers have been concerned with writing programs rather than with building ever more novel forms of computing hardware. The general-purpose machine is already here, and such a machine can be programmed to simulate any specific kind of information processor we like. On the face of it then, the most promising approach to the simulation of cognitive processes would seem to be by means of artfully designed programs running on general-purpose machines. In the next section we shall explore some of the results of this fertile approach.

Suggested Readings

Weizenbaum, Jospeh, *Computer Power and Human Reason* (San Francisco: Freeman, 1976); see especially chapters 2 and 3.

Raphael, Bertram, *The Thinking Computer: Mind inside Matter* (San Francisco: Freeman 1976).

Newell, Alan, and Simon, Herbert, "Computer Science as Empirical Inquiry: Symbols and Search," in *Mind Design*, ed. J. Haugeland (Montgomery, VT: Bradford, 1981; Cambridge, MA: MIT Press).

2. Programming Intelligence: The Piecemeal Approach

A naive approach to programming intelligence might suppose that what is needed is that some programming genius, on some particularly inspired occasion, spend the night in furious creation and emerge in the morning with The Secret, in the form of a program, which when run on the nearest available machine, produces another consciousness just like you and me. Though appealing, this is comic-book stuff. It is naive in assuming that there is a single, uniform phenomenon to be captured, and naive in assuming that there is a unique hidden essence responsible for it.

Even a casual glance at the animal kingdom will reveal that intelligence comes in many thousands of different grades, and that in different creatures it is constituted by different skills, concerns, and strategies, all reflecting differences in their physiological construction and evolutionary history. To take a popular example, in many of its aspects the intelligence of a dolphin must differ substantially from the intelligence of a human. On the output side, the dolphin has no arms, hands, and fingers for intricate manipulation; neither does it need to maintain itself in an unstable vertical position in a permanent gravitational field. It thus has no need for the specific control mechanisms that, in a human, administer these vital matters. On the input side, the dolphin's principal sense is sonar echolocation, which provides a window onto the world very different from that of vision. Even so, the dolphin has processing mechanisms that make its sonar comparable to vision in overall power. For example, sonar is blind to color; on the other hand, it reveals to the dolphin the internal structure of perceived bodies, since everything is 'transparent' to sound in some degree. Filtering out such information from complex echoes, however, presents a dolphin's brain with problems different from those that confront the human visual cortex, and no doubt the dolphin has specialized brain mechanisms or neural procedures for routinely solving them.

These major differences in input/output processing may well involve other differences at deeper levels, and we can begin to appreciate that the intelligence of each type of creature is probably unique to that species. And what makes it unique is the specific blend of special-purpose information-processing mechanisms that evolution has in them knit together. This helps us to appreciate that our own intelligence must be a rope of many different strands. To simulate it, therefore, will require that we knit together similar threads in similar ways. And doing that will require that we first construct the threads. For this reason, AI researchers have tended to single out some one aspect of intelligence, and then concentrate on simulating that aspect. As a matter of strategy, problems of integration can temporarily be put aside.

**Purposive Behavior
and Problem Solving**

Many things fall under this broad
heading—hunting prey, playing
chess, building towers of blocks—
in general, anything where the activities of the agent can be seen as
an attempt to achieve a specific end or goal. A maximally simple case
would be a homing torpedo, or a heat-seeking missile. These will move
steering fins and engage in twists and turns in such a way as to remain
fixed on the evasive target. They can seem fiercely single-minded if
one is on your tail, but in a calm moment there is little temptation to
ascribe any real intelligence to them, since they have a unique response
to each evasive action, one keyed directly to the 'target-deviation-from-
dead-center' measurement by the missile's sensor. Such systems are
not irrelevant to understanding animal behavior—mosquitoes apparently home, with equal simplicity, on increasing carbon dioxide gradients
(exhaled breath)—but we want more from AI than the intelligence of
a mosquito.

What of a case where the range of possible responses to any perceived
gap between present-state and goal-state is much larger, and what if
a useful choice from among those responses requires some problem
solving on the part of the agent? That sounds more like the business
of real intelligence. Intriguingly, a considerable variety of existing programs can meet this condition, and some of them produce complex
behavior that, in a human, would be regarded as highly intelligent.

Starting with the simple cases, consider the game of tic-tac-toe, or
× 's and O's (figure 6.2), and consider the procedures a computer might
exploit to maximize its chances of winning or at least drawing against
any other player. Supposing that the computer goes first with × 's,
there are 9 possible moves it could make. For each of these there are

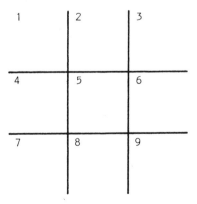

Figure 6.2

8 possible countermoves for the O-player. And for each of these, there are 7 possible responses by the computer. And so on. On the simplest reckoning, there are $9 \times 8 \times 7 \times \cdots \times 2$ ($= 9! = 362,880$) distinct ways of filling up the game matrix. (There are somewhat less than this many complete games, since most games end when three-in-a-row is achieved, and before the matrix is full.) We can represent these possibilities as a *game tree* (figure 6.3).

This game tree is much too large to fit more than a sampling of it onto a page, but it is not too large for a suitably programmed computer swiftly to explore every single branch and note whether it ends in a win, loss, or draw for ×. This information can inform its choice of moves at each stage of the game. Let us say that any branch of the tree confronting × is a "bad branch" if on the *next* move the O-player has a game-ending move that wins for O. And let us say further that any branch confronting × is also a bad branch if on the next move the O-player has a move that will leave × confronting only bad branches. With this recursive definition in hand, and identifying the bad terminal branches first, the computer can then work back down the tree and identify *all* of the bad branches. If we further program it so that, at each stage of the actual game, it never chooses one of the

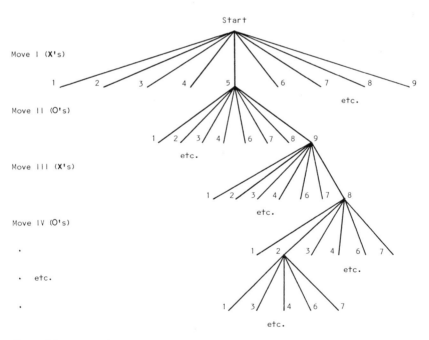

Figure 6.3

bad branches it has thus identified, and always chooses a winning move over a draw, then the computer will never lose a game! The best one can hope to do against it is draw, and two computers thus programmed will draw every game against each other.

To illustrate these points briefly, consider the specific game ×—5, O—9, ×—8, O—2, ×—7, O—3, ×—6, O—1. And let us pick up the game after move IV, with the matrix as in figure 6.4.

You may pencil in the last four moves, if you wish, and witness ×'s downfall. If we now look at a portion of the search tree extending from O's move at IV (figure 6.5), we can see why × should not have chosen square 7 on move V. From there, O has a move (into square 3) that leaves × confronting *only* bad branches. × must choose 1, 4, or 6, on move VII, and all three leave O with a winning choice on the very next move. All three are therefore bad branches. Therefore, ×'s branch to square 7 at move V is *also* a bad branch, since it permits O, on the next move, to leave × staring at all bad branches. In light of this, we can appreciate that × should not go to 7 at move V. So can our programmed computer, and it will therefore avoid the mistake just explored. And all others, wherever placed in the tree.

Thus we have here a case where the programmed machine has a goal (to win, or at least draw), a range of possible responses to each circumstance in which it may find itself, and a procedure for solving, at each stage, the problem of which among them is best suited to achieve that goal. (If two or more are equally good, then we can instruct it just to choose the first on the list or to 'flip a coin' with some randomizing subroutine.)

The particular strategy outlined is an instance of what is called the *brute force* approach to problem solving: from the basic description of

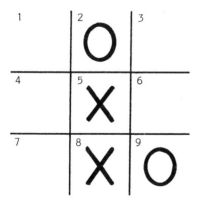

Figure 6.4

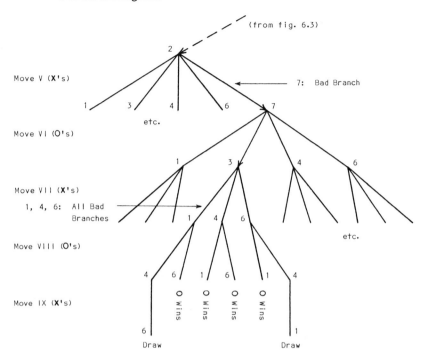

Figure 6.5

the problem, the computer grows a *search tree* that comprehends every relevant possibility, and it conducts an exhaustive search for the branch or branches that constitute a solution. This is called an *exhaustive look-ahead*. For problems that have a solution (not all do), this approach works beautifully, given that sufficient 'force' is available. It constitutes an effective procedure, or *algorithm*, for identifying the best moves.

'Force' here means speed and memory capacity on the part of the machine: sufficient force to construct and search the relevant tree. Unfortunately, many of the problems that confront real intelligence involve search trees that are beyond the reach of feasible machines and the brute force approach. Even for tic-tac-toe, the specific strategy described requires high speed and a large memory. And for more demanding games, the approach quickly becomes unworkable.

Consider chess. A demanding endeavor, no doubt, but no more demanding than the social 'games' humans routinely play. On average, a player at any stage of a chess game must choose from among 30 or so legal moves. And each move will make possible some 30 or so responses from his opponent. The first two moves alone, then, are a pair chosen from about 30^2 (= 30×30 = 900) possible pairs. If an average game involves about 40 moves by each player, for a total of 80, then the number of distinct possible average games is 30 to the 80th power, or about 10^{118}. The relevant game tree, therefore, will have about 10^{118} branches. This is a preposterously large number. A million computers each examining a million branches per second would still take 10^{100} (a one followed by 100 zeros) *years* to examine the entire tree. Clearly, this approach to chess playing is not going to work.

The problem encountered here is an instance of *combinatorial explosion*, and it means that a chess-playing program cannot hope to use an algorithm to identify the guaranteed-best possible moves. It must fall back on *heuristic* procedures. That is, it must exploit 'rules of thumb' to distinguish the merely promising moves from the not-so-promising ones. Consider how this can work. If we write the program so that the computer does not try to look ahead 40 moves, but only 4 moves (= 2 for each player) at any stage in the game, then the relevant search tree has only 30^4, or 800,000, branches. This is small enough for existing machines to search in a reasonable time. But what does it search for, if it cannot search for ultimate victory? Here we try to provide the computer with intermediate goals that (a) it *can* effectively identify, and that (b) offer some *probability* that if they are repeatedly achieved, then ultimate victory will thereby also be achieved.

For example, we can assign numbers to the loss of specific pieces, in proportion to their general importance; and any potential exchange of pieces with an opponent can be assigned an overall positive or negative value by the computer, depending on who loses and how much. The computer can further guide its choice of moves by assigning a certain positive value to having its pieces 'in control of the center' (= having pieces in a position to make captures in the center portion of the board). A further value can be assigned to potential moves that attack the opponent's king, since that is a necessary condition for victory. And so forth.

We can write the program so that the computer adds these factors, for each considered move, and then chooses the move with the highest aggregate value. In this way, we can at least get the computer to *play* a recognizable game of chess, which is impossible on the brute force approach, since the machine is paralyzed by the immensity of the task.

The fact is, chess-playing programs using heuristics such as these, and others more cunning, have been written that will beat the pants off anybody except those few devotees at the master level, and even here they perform respectably. (Simpler, but still impressive, programs have been commercially available for several years now, embodied in 'electronic chessboards'. AI has made it into the marketplace.) Such intricately tuned behavior is an impressive display, even by human standards of intelligence. Heuristic-guided look-ahead may not be infallible, but it can still be very powerful.

A strategy different from exhaustive look-ahead and heuristic-guided partial look-ahead is represented by another class of programs that simulate problem solving and purposive behavior. Instead of addressing a goal by first considering every possible move within the computer's power, and then every further possible move from there, and so forth, in hopes that some branch of this exploding tree will eventually make contact with the goal, the computer can start at the other end of the problem. It can begin by considering all of the possible circumstances it can consider, in which *one* further move on its part would secure the goal. There need not be many of these—perhaps only one. These possible circumstances then become intermediate goals, and the computer can repeat its explorations into possible ways to secure one or more of *them*. This process is repeated until the computer finally identifies some circumstance that it does have the power to bring about immediately. The computer then makes this move, and, in reverse order, all the others in the means-end chain that it has constructed, thus achieving its original and ultimate goal. This strategy need not always be more efficient than exhaustive look-ahead, but if there are a great many moves the computer might make at the outset, and only a very few that lead toward achieving the goal, this approach can be far swifter.

The program STRIPS (Stanford Research Institute Problem Solver) is capable of this strategy. A mobile robot with the descriptive name of Shakey was remotely controlled by a computer running STRIPS, and this system could be set various goals, to be achieved in an environment of several rooms connected by doors and populated with various large boxes. Given information as to the disposition of the rooms, connecting doors, boxes, and Shakey itself, and given a goal of the form "Bring it about that the box in room 3 is put into room 7", Shakey (or rather, STRIPS) would construct on its own and execute a sequence of behaviors that would bring this about.

Learning We should also note two ways in which *learning* can be displayed by programs of the sort at issue. The first and simplest is just a matter of saving, in memory, solutions already achieved. When the same problem is confronted again, the solution can be instantly recalled from memory and used directly, instead of being laboriously re-solved each time. A lesson, once learned, is remembered. Purposive behavior that was halting at first can thus become smooth and unhesitating.

The second way can be illustrated in the case of a heuristic-guided chess program. If we write the program so that the computer keeps a record of its win/loss ratio, we can have it try new weightings for its several heuristics if it finds itself losing at an unacceptable rate. Suppose, for example, that the "attack your opponent's king" heuristic is weighted too heavily, initially, and that the machine loses games regularly because of repeated kamikaze attacks on the opposing king. After noting its losses, the computer could try adjusting each of its weightings in turn, to see whether a better win/loss ratio results. In the long run, the overweighted heuristic would be reweighted downward, and the quality of the machine's game would improve. In something like the way you or I might, the computer learns to play a stronger game.

Clearly these two strategies will reproduce some of what we ordinarily call learning. There is far more to learning, however, than the mere storage of acquired information. In both of the strategies described, the machine represents the 'learned' information within the scheme of concepts and categories supplied by its original program. In neither case does the machine generate *new* concepts and categories with which to analyze and manipulate incoming information. It can manipulate the old categories, and form a variety of combinations of them, but conceptual innovation is limited to combinatorial activity within the original framework.

This is an extremely conservative form of learning, as we can appreciate when we consider the learning undergone by a small child in the first two years of its life, or by the scientific community in the course of a century. Large-scale conceptual change—the generation of a genuinely new categorial framework that displaces the old framework entirely—is characteristic of both processes. We cannot pretend to have solved the problem of learning until we have solved the problem of conceptual change.

This more profound type of learning is much more difficult to simulate or recreate than are the simpler types discussed above, for it will require of us some way of representing knowledge and information at a level *beneath* the level of linguistically expressible concepts, a level whose elements can in some way be combined or articulated to form any of a vast range of alternative possible concepts. Such a level of representation must also be sensitive and responsive to the subsequent performance of the overall system, so that successful concepts can be distinguished from those that are useless and confused.

This problem has appeared almost insuperable until only very recently. Happily, new approaches to the representation and manipulation of large amounts of information have recently produced some very striking 'learning procedures', and these have captured a good deal of current attention. However, they are designed to be implemented, at least ideally, on computing machines of a construction very different from those described a few pages ago, and to describe them at just this point would be a digression. They resurface in chapter 7.

Vision

If equipped with optical sensors, could a suitably programmed computer *see*? At a simple level of optical-information processing, the answer is clearly yes. Publishing houses often use such a system in the course of setting a book into type. An author's original typescript is 'read' by a system that scans each character in sequence and records its identity on tape. Another computer uses that tape to run the typesetting machine. Character-recognition scanners can be very simple. A lens system projects a black-and-white image of the character onto a grid of photosensitive elements (figure 6.6). Selected squares of the grid are largely occluded by the character's image, and the scanning device sends a coded list of them all to the computer. The relevant program then has the computer compare that list to each of many standard lists in its memory—one for each standard character. It singles out the stored list that agrees with the received list at the greatest number of points, and identifies the scanned character accordingly. All of this at lightning speed, of course.

Plainly, this system is inflexible and can easily be victimized. Unusual character fonts will produce chronic misidentifications. And if the system is fed images of faces, or of animals, it will carry right on as before, identifying them as sundry letters and numerals. Just the same, these failings parallel obvious features of our own visual system. We too tend

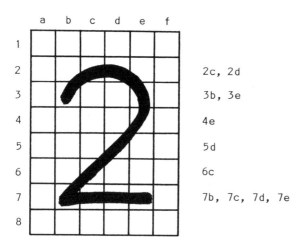

Figure 6.6

to interpret what we see in terms of familiar or expected categories, and we often fail even to notice novelty unless put actively on guard against it.

Character recognition represents only the raw beginnings of machine vision, however, not its pinnacle. Consider the more general problem of identifying and locating objects in three-dimensional space, using no more data than is presented in a two-dimensional array of variously illuminated dots: this is called an *intensity array*, and a television picture provides a familiar example. Except for having many more elements, and graded values for each element, it is just a fancy case of our earlier grid for character recognition.

You and I have retinas that function as our intensity arrays, and we can solve the relevant problems with ease, seeing specific arrangements of objects on the strength of specific retinal intensity arrays. We are unaware of the 'problem' of interpretation and unaware of the processing within us that solves it. But such competence is a real challenge to the programmer, since it reflects substantial intelligence on the part of the visual system.

This is because visual representations are always and endlessly *ambiguous*. Many different external circumstances are strictly consistent with any given two-dimensional intensity array. That is to say, different circumstances can 'look' roughly or even exactly the same, as a normal penny, tilted slightly, looks the same as a truly elliptical coin. Any visual system must be able to disambiguate scenes in a reasonable way, to find the most *likely* interpretation given the data. As well, some scenes are more complex than others: the 'correct' interpretation may require concepts that the system does not even possess. This suggests that vision, like intelligence itself, comes in grades. Fortunately, this allows us to approach the simple cases first.

Consider a specific intensity array: think of a television picture of several large boxes piled in a jumble. Sudden changes in the intensity of reflected light mark the edges of each box, and a program sensitive to such changes can construct from them a line sketch of the several boxes and their relative positions. From here, a program sensitive to the ways in which edges meet to form corners/sides/entire volumes (such as Guzman's SEE program) can correctly divine how many boxes are there and in what relative positions. Such programs function well, for highly artificial environments that contain only plane-sided solids, but many ambiguities remain beyond their resolution, and they come completely unstuck when presented with a rocky beach or a leafy glen.

More recent programs exploit the information contained in *continuous* changes in intensity—think of the way the light is distributed on a sphere or a cylinder—to fund hypotheses about a much wider range of objects. And artificial stereopsis is also being explored. The subtle differences between a pair of two-dimensional intensity arrays taken from two slightly different positions (such as the images on your right and left retinas) contain potentially decisive information on the contours and relative spatial positions of items in the scene. An algorithm has already been written that will recover the three-dimensional information hidden in the stereo pair displayed in figure 6.7.

Place a business-size envelope vertically between the two squares, and center your nose and forehead on the near edge of the envelope so that each eye sees but one image. Or better yet, make a pair of paper binoculars by rolling up two letter-size sheets of paper into a pair of long tubes. Hold them in parallel, with one end of each close to the page, so that each eye looks straight down through a tube and sees but one square centered in the circular opening. Allow your visual system a few minutes to fuse the left and right images into a single clearly focused image (be patient), and you can watch as your own highly skilled algorithm finds the same information.

A chronic problem with machine vision is that, since vision itself involves intelligence, and since what any creature can see in a given situation is heavily dependent on what concepts it already has and on what knowledge it already possesses, the creation of high-powered artificial visual systems is contingent upon the creation of high-powered intelligence generally, and upon the creation of systems that possess very extensive knowledge bases to give direction to their perceptual processing. This is neither surprising nor particularly disappointing, but it does illustrate the limitations of a purely piecemeal approach to the simulation of cognitive faculties.

Figure 6.7 Reprinted with permission from D. Marr and T. Poggio, "Cooperative Computation of Stereo Disparity," *Science*, vol. 194 (1976), 283–286. Copyright 1976 by the AAAS.

Natural-Language Manipulation   Another area in which the lack of a truly extensive knowledge base has frustrated researchers is the area of natural-language comprehension and production. For many reasons, it is desirable to be able to converse with computers in ordinary English, and natural-language manipulation is a central element of human intelligence in any case, worthy of simulation in its own right. Structural insight on the part of linguists and computational cunning on the part of programmers have produced programs that handle the syntactic structures of English well enough, even the more complex ones; but the *semantic* part of the problem has been less tractable. As it happens, one can do a surprising amount by the manipulation of syntax alone. Consider Weizenbaum's famous early program, ELIZA, which simulates a psychotherapist with whom the 'patient' converses via typewriter. The following is an excerpt from such an exchange, with the computer's responses in uppercase (from Weizenbaum, 1976):

Men are all alike.

IN WHAT WAY

They're always bugging us about something or other.

CAN YOU THINK OF A SPECIFIC EXAMPLE

Well, my boyfriend made me come here.

YOUR BOYFRIEND MADE YOU COME HERE

He says I'm depressed much of the time.

I AM SORRY TO HEAR YOU ARE DEPRESSED

It's true. I am unhappy.

DO YOU THINK COMING HERE WILL HELP YOU NOT TO BE UNHAPPY

I need some help, that much seems certain.

WHAT WOULD IT MEAN TO YOU IF YOU GOT SOME HELP

Perhaps I could learn to get along with my mother.

TELL ME MORE ABOUT YOUR FAMILY

My mother takes care of me.

WHO ELSE IN YOUR FAMILY TAKES CARE OF YOU

My father.

YOUR FATHER

You are like my father in some ways.

WHAT RESEMBLANCE DO YOU SEE

You are not very aggressive, but I think you don't want me to notice that.

WHAT MAKES YOU THINK I AM NOT VERY AGGRESSIVE

You don't argue with me.

WHY DO YOU THINK I DONT ARGUE WITH YOU

You are afraid of me.

DOES IT PLEASE YOU TO BELIEVE I AM AFRAID OF YOU

My father is afraid of everybody.

WHAT ELSE COMES TO MIND WHEN YOU THINK OF YOUR
FATHER

Bullies.

DOES THAT HAVE ANYTHING TO DO WITH THE FACT THAT
YOUR BOYFRIEND MADE YOU COME HERE

⋮

In this conversation, the computer, running ELIZA, gives the eerie
impression of real understanding. But in fact it has none. The responses
are largely constructed from the patient's own sentences, by simple
transformations, and from a stock of standard question forms tailored
to key words from the patient ("depressed", "like", and so on). ELIZA
has no conception of what a father, a brother, or unhappiness is. It
has no concept of these things, no understanding of what these words
mean. Which just goes to show how surprisingly little understanding
is required to engage successfully in many standard forms of
conversation.

A much more impressive program is Winograd's SHRDLU, which
handles semantics as well as syntax, and manipulates the elements in
the (simulated) block world that is all that it knows. Its syntax is very
sophisticated, and the program embodies some systematic information
about the properties of the bodies that inhabit its world. Crudely, it
knows, a little, what it is talking about. As a result, it can draw useful
inferences and divine real relations, a talent that is reflected in the
much more complex and keenly focused conversations one can have
with it. Conversations must be restricted to the block world, however,
and to those narrow aspects it encompasses. SHRDLU does not have
an empty knowledge base, but its base is still less than microscopic
compared with our own.

In a nutshell, the problem is that to understand natural language at
the human level requires that one have an overall *knowledge* of the
world that is comparable to what a human possesses (recall the holistic
theory of meaning, the 'network theory', discussed in chapter 3.3), and
we have not yet solved the problem of how to represent and store such

an enormous knowledge base in a fashion that would make access and manipulation feasible. Related to this is a deeper problem. We have not yet solved the problem of how such global amounts of knowledge can even be *acquired*. How entire conceptual frameworks are generated, modified, and then thrown away in favor of new and more sophisticated frameworks; how such frameworks are evaluated as revealing or misleading, as true or false; none of this is understood at all well. And very little of it has even been addressed by AI.

These problems are the traditional province of inductive logic, epistemology, and semantic theory, for philosophers. And they are also the province of developmental psychology and learning theory, for psychologists. A collective assault seems required, for the phenomena to be understood are as complex and difficult as any we have ever faced. No doubt patience is also required here, for we cannot expect to create in a mere few decades what it has taken the evolutionary process three billion years to make.

Self Consciousness   The reader will have noted that none of the simulations here discussed addresses the issue of self-consciousness. Perhaps visual and tactile sensors, plus fancy programming, provide a computer with some 'awareness' of the external world, but they promise little or nothing in the direction of self-consciousness. This is not to be wondered at. If self-consciousness consists in the introspective apprehension of one's own high-level cognitive processes, then there is little or no point to trying to simulate the *apprehension* of such processes until *they* have been successfully simulated. A full-scale assault on self-perception can perhaps be postponed until AI has constructed some 'selves' truly worthy of explicit reflexive perception. Some preliminary work has already proved necessary, however. Proprioception—awareness of the position of one's limbs in space—is one form of self-perception, and for obvious reasons the development of computer-controlled robot arms has required that the computer be given some systematic means of sensing the position and motion of its own arm, and of representing this information in a way that is continuously useful to it. Perhaps this already constitutes a primitive and isolated form of self-consciousness.

Finally, we must not be misled by the term "simulation" to dismiss out of hand the prospects of this overall approach to the problem of conscious intelligence, for the simulation at issue can be *functional* simulation in the strongest possible sense. According to those AI theorists who take the human computational system as their model, there need be no difference between your computational procedures and the computational procedures of a machine simulation, no difference beyond the particular physical substance that sustains those activities. In you, it is organic material; in the computer, it woud be metals and semi-conductors. But *this* difference is no more relevant to the question of conscious intelligence than is a difference in blood type, or skin color, or metabolic chemistry, claims the (functionalist) AI theorist. If machines do come to simulate all of our internal cognitive activities, to the last computational detail, to deny them the status of genuine persons would be nothing but a new form of racism.

Some Chronic Problems   The preceding section was upbeat in its evaluation of the abstract prospects of AI, but there are certain recurrent difficulties that have frustrated the research program of traditional or 'program writing' AI, and it behooves us to acknowledge them and to speculate about their significance.

One puzzling fact about the results of AI research is that there are certain kinds of tasks, such as number crunching, theorem proving, and list searching, which standard computers do very swiftly and very well, while the human brain does them only slowly and comparatively badly. On the other hand, there are certain kinds of tasks, such as facial recognition, scene apprehension, sensorimotor coordination, and learning, which humans and other animals do swiftly and well, but which even the fastest computers running the most sophisticated programs do only slowly and rather poorly.

More specifically, you can recognize a photo of your best friend's face, in any of a wide range of poses, in less than half a second. But such a recognitional achievement still eludes the best pattern-recognition programs available, and even strongly simplified versions of recognitional problems like this take minutes of furious computer processing, or more, before any solution to the problem is reached.

For a second example, you can learn to hit a tennis ball back over the net in not more than ten or fifteen tries. But the sensorimotor coordination required to guide the behavior of a skeletal and muscular system as complicated as the human body, in real time, is still well beyond the capacity of current AI. And the idea of a program that could *learn* to make such a system perform tennis returns, and do it in less than fifteen tries, is a prospect even more distant.

A Recent Diagnosis   Why is it that the brain is so much better than even the most cunningly programmed machines at performing certain familiar tasks, and so much poorer than even the simplest computers at performing others? The answer would seem to lie in the radically different kinds of physical and computational architecture displayed by the two kinds of information-processing systems. Although standard computers are indeed 'general-purpose' machines, in the sense that they can simulate any possible information-processing system, there are many kinds of systems whose simulation requires *enormous* amounts of time-consuming activity from the central processing unit of a standard computer. Biological brains appear to be such awkward-to-simulate systems. They are simulatable in principle, but only at the expense of settling for a computer simulation that ends up solving the relevant problem or performing the desired activities at a speed very much slower than the brain—perhaps millions or billions of times slower.

What accounts for such a wide difference in speed? The problem would seem to lie in the processing 'bottleneck' of the CPU in the standard general-purpose machine. The CPU of such machines is typically a very brisk worker, performing something on the order of a million (10^6) distinct computations per second. Considered in isolation, this is impressive. But however fast it works, it can still do only one computation at a time, and many problems, such as the learning and recognition tasks described above, require for their solution considerably more than a *billion* (10^9) distinct computational steps. Since each one has to be performed by the CPU, one after the other in a carefully orchestrated serial fashion, clearly the machine will take at least ($10^9/10^6 =$) 1000 seconds, or over a quarter of an hour, to solve such a problem. That is a long time by biological standards. A mouse who cannot recognize cats faster than that is doomed to be lunch.

The brain, by contrast, does not have a CPU in which all of its computations are confined and through which all information must pass. Brains appear to have a physical and computational structure that is radically different from typical computing machines, a structure that allows for billions of simple computations to be performed *simultaneously*. Since each of these computations is very simple, it is executed swiftly by only one of the billions of distinct cells that the brain contains, and it is all done in such a fashion that their collective output embodies the completed solution to the problem at hand.

Here there is no computational bottleneck through which all of the relevant bits of information must squeeze, one after the other in single file. Since each brain cell simultaneously contributes only one computation to the overall process, the entire operation can be completed in a single pass through the relevant network of brain cells. And that single pass need take no more than 1/100th of a second, since it goes through every cell in the network at exactly the same time. Thus the brain, even the mouse's brain, can perform complex recognitional tasks in a flash.

This different style of information processing is called *parallel processing*, in contrast to the *serial processing* displayed by standard computing machines. What it provides is a truly enormous advantage in the speed with which certain kinds of computationally intensive problems can be solved. This speed advantage has made parallel processing the focus of much recent attention among researchers in AI and Cognitive Science, but speed is not the only feature that recommends it. Parallel processors have some very interesting computational properties, such as functional persistence despite damage to the system, and the capacity for generalizing acquired knowledge to new situations. All of this is very exciting, especially since the architecture of such systems resembles that of the brain more closely than does the serial architecture of standard computing machines.

This new style of research in AI and Cognitive Science goes by the name of *Connectionism*, or *PDP* research. The former term was coined to indicate that computations can be performed not just by central processors, but also by the intricate system of connections within which a large number of extremely *simple* processing units are joined. The second term is an acronym for "Parallel Distributed Processing", which expression connotes the same computational idea. Some properties of these systems, and some results of this research, will be examined toward the end of the next chapter. Since PDP systems are to some degree biologically inspired, they will be most conveniently addressed after we have learned something about the structure of the brain.

Suggested Readings

Boden, Margaret, *Artificial Intelligence and Natural Man* (New York: Harvester Press, 1977).

Dennett, Daniel, "Artificial Intelligence as Philosophy and as Psychology," in *Philosophical Perspectives on Artificial Intelligence*, ed. M. Ringle (New Jersey: Humanities Press, 1979). Reprinted in Daniel Dennett, *Brainstorms* (Montgomery, VT: Bradford, 1978; Cambridge, MA: MIT Press).

Winston, P. H., and Brown, R. H., *Artificial Intelligence: An MIT Perspective*, vols. I and II (Cambridge, MA: MIT Press, 1979).

Marr, D., and Poggio, T., "Cooperative Computation of Stereo Disparity," *Science*, vol. 194 (1976).

Dreyfus, Hubert, *What Computers Can't Do: The Limits of Artificial Intelligence*, revised edition (New York: Harper and Row, 1979).

Haugeland, J., *Artificial Intelligence: The Very Idea* (Cambridge, MA: MIT Press, 1985).

Holland, J., Holyoak, K., Nisbett, R., and Thagard, P., *Induction: Processes of Inference, Learning, and Discovery* (Cambridge, MA: MIT Press, 1986).

Rumelhart, D., and McClelland, J., *Parallel Distributed Processing: Essays in the Microstructure of Cognition* (Cambridge, MA: MIT Press, 1986).

Chapter 7
Neuroscience

1. Neuroanatomy: The Evolutionary Background

Near the surface of the earth's oceans, between three and four billion years ago, the sun-driven process of purely chemical evolution produced some *self-replicating* molecular structures. From the molecular bits and pieces in their immediate environment, these complex molecules could catalyze a sequence of bonding reactions that yielded exact copies of themselves. With respect to achieving large populations, the capacity for self-replication is plainly an explosive advantage. Population growth is limited, however, by the availability of the right bits and pieces in the molecular soup surrounding, and by the various forces in the environment that tend to break down these heroic structures before they can replicate themselves. Among competing self-replicating molecules, therefore, the competitive advantage will go to those specific molecular structures that induce, not just their own replication, but the formation of structures that protect them against external predations, and the formation of mechanisms that produce needed molecular parts by the chemical manipulation of environmental molecules that are unusable directly.

The *cell* is the triumphant example of this solution. It has an outer membrane to protect the intricate structures within, and complex metabolic pathways that process outside material into internal structure. At the center of this complex system sits a carefully coded DNA molecule, the director of cellular activity and the winner of the competition described. Its cells now dominate the earth. All competitors have been swept aside by their phenomenal success, save for the residual viruses, which alone pursue the earlier strategy, now as parasitic invaders upon cellular success. With the emergence of the cell, we have what fits our standard conception of *life*: a self-maintaining, self-replicating, energy-using system.

The emergence of conscious intelligence, as one aspect of living matter, must be seen against the background of biological evolution in general. We here pick up the story after it is already well along: after multicelled organisms have made their appearance, close to one billion years ago. Significant intelligence requires a nervous system, and single-celled organisms such as algae or bacteria cannot have a nervous system, since a nervous system is itself an organization of many cells. The main advantage of being a multicelled organism is that individual cells can be specialized. Some can form a tough outer wall, within which other cells can enjoy an environment more stable and beneficial than the ocean at large. Those cloistered cells can exercise their own specializations: digestion of food, transport of nutrients to other cells, contraction and elongation to produce movement, sensitivity to key environmental factors (the presence of food or predators), and so on. The result of such organization can be a system that is more durable than any of its parts, and far more likely to succeed in reproducing itself than is any one of its single-celled competitors.

The coordination of these specialized parts requires *communication* between cells, however, and some additional specializations must address this important task. It is no use having muscles if their contractions cannot be coordinated to produce useful locomotion, or mastication, or elimination. Sensory cells are useless if their information cannot be conveyed to the motor system. And so on. Purely chemical communication is useful for some purposes: growth and repair is regulated in this way, with messenger cells broadcasting specific chemicals throughout the body, to which selected cells respond. But this is too slow and too unspecific a means of communication for most purposes.

Fortunately, cells themselves have the basic features needed to serve as communicative links. Most cells maintain a tiny voltage difference—a *polarization*—across the inner and outer surfaces of their enveloping cell membranes. An appropriate disturbance at any point on the membrane can cause a sudden *de*polarization at that point and, like the collapse of a train of dominoes stood precariously on end, the depolarization will spread some distance along the surface of the cell. After this depolarization, the cell gamely pumps itself back up again. In most cells, the depolarization pulse attenuates and dies in a short distance, but in others it does not. Conjoin this convenient property of cells with the fact that single cells can assume greatly elongated shapes—filaments of a meter or more in extreme cases—and you have the perfect elements for a communication system: specialized nerve cells that conduct electrochemical impulses over long distances at high speed.

Further specializations are possible. Some cells depolarize upon receipt of physical pressure, others upon changes in temperature, others upon sudden changes in illumination, and still others upon receipt of suitable impulses from other cells. With the articulation of such cells we have the beginnings of the sensory and central nervous system, and we open a new chapter in the evolutionary drama.

**The Development of
Nervous Systems**

The appearance of nervous control systems should not be seen as something miraculous. To appreciate just how easily a control system can come to characterize an entire species, consider an imaginary snail-like creature that lives on the ocean bottom. This species must come partway out of its shell to feed, and it withdraws into its shell only when the creature is sated, or when some external body makes direct contact with it, as when a predator attacks. Many of these creatures are lost to predators, despite the tactile withdrawal reflex, since many are killed at the very first contact. Even so, the species' population is stable, being in equilibrium with the population of predators.

As it happens, every snail of this species has a band of light-sensitive cells on the back of its head. In this there is nothing remarkable. Many types of cells happen to be light sensitive to some degree, and the light sensitivity of these is an incidental feature of the species, a feature that does nothing. Suppose now that an individual snail, because of a small mutation in the coding of its initial DNA, has grown more than the usual number of nerve cells connecting its skin surface to its withdrawal muscles. In particular, it is alone among its conspecifics in having connections from its light-sensitive cells to its withdrawal muscles. Sudden changes in the general illumination thus cause a prompt withdrawal into its shell.

This incidental feature in this one individual would be of no significance in many environments, a mere idiosyncratic 'twitch' of no use whatever. In the snails' actual environment, however, sudden changes in illumination are most often caused by *predators* swimming directly overhead. Our mutant individual, therefore, possesses an 'early-warning system' that permits it to withdraw safely *before* the predator gets to take a bite. Its chances of survival, and of repeated reproduction, are thus much greater than the chances of its unequipped fellows. And since its novel possession is the result of a genetic mutation, many of its offspring will share in it. Their chances of survival and reproduction are similarly enhanced. Clearly this feature will swiftly come to dominate the snail population. Of such small and fortuitous events are great changes made.

Further exploitation is easily conceived. If by genetic mutation a light-sensitive surface becomes curved into a hemispherical pit, its selectively illuminated portions then provide *directional* information about light sources and occlusions, information that can drive directional

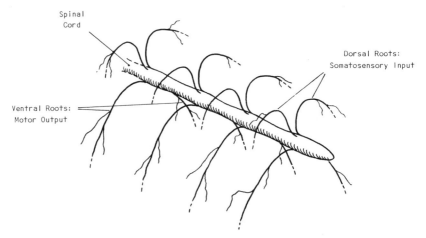

Spinal
Cord

Dorsal Roots:
Somatosensory Input

Ventral Roots:
Motor Output

Figure 7.1

motor responses. In a mobile creature like a fish, this affords a major advantage, both as hunter and as prey. Once widely distributed, a hemispherical pit can be transformed into a nearly spherical pit with only a pinhole opening left to the outside. Such a pinhole will form a feeble *image* of the outside world on the light-sensitive surface. Transparent cells can come to cover that pinhole, functioning first as protection, and later as a lens for superior images. All the while, increased innervation (concentration of nerve cells) in the 'retina' is rewarded by superior information to conduct elsewhere in the nervous system. By such simple and advantageous stages is the 'miraculous' eye assembled. And this reconstruction is not sheer speculation. A contemporary creature can be found for each one of the developmental stages cited.

In general, our reconstruction of the evolutionary history of nervous systems is based on three sorts of studies: fossil remains, current creatures of primitive construction, and nervous development in embryos. Being so soft, nervous tissue does not itself fossilize, but we can trace nervous structure in ancient vertebrates (animals with a backbone) from the chambers, passages, and clefts found in the skulls and spinal columns of fossil animals. This is a very reliable guide to size and gross structure, but fine detail is entirely missing. For detail, we turn to the existing animal kingdom, which contains thousands of species whose nervous systems appear to have changed very little in the course of millions of years. Here we have to be careful, since "simple" does not necessarily mean "primitive", but we can construct very plausible developmental 'trees' from such study. Embryological development provides a fascinating check on both studies, since some (only *some*) of any creature's evolutionary history is written in the developmental sequence by which DNA articulates a fertilized egg cell into a creature of that type. Putting all three together, the following history emerges.

The most primitive vertebrates possessed an elongated central *ganglion* (cluster of cells) running the length of the spine, which was connected to the rest of the body by two functionally and physically distinct sets of fibers (figure 7.1). The *somatosensory* fibers brought information about muscle activity and tactile stimulation to the central cord, and the *motor* fibers took command impulses from it to the body's muscle tissues. The central cord itself functioned to coordinate the body's many muscles with one another to produce a coherent swimming motion, and to coordinate such motion with sensed circumstance, to provide flight from tactile assault or a searching motion to relieve an empty stomach.

In later creatures this primitive *spinal cord* has acquired an elongation at the front end and three swellings where the population and density of nerve cells reaches new levels. This primitive brain or *brain stem* can be divided into the *forebrain, midbrain,* and *hindbrain* (figure 7.2). The nervous network of the small forebrain was then devoted to the processing of olfactory stimuli; the midbrain processed visual and auditory information; and the hindbrain specialized in still more sophisticated coordination of motor activity. The brains of contemporary fishes remain at this stage, with the midbrain the dominant structure.

In more advanced animals such as the amphibians and the reptiles, it is the forebrain that comes to dominate the brain stem's anatomy, and to assume a central role in processing all of the sensory modalities, not just olfaction (figure 7.3). In many animals, absolute size also increases, and with it the absolute numbers of cells in what is already a complex and quasiautonomous control network. That network had much to do: many dinosaurs were swift bipedal carnivores that pursued distant

Brain Stem (Primitive)

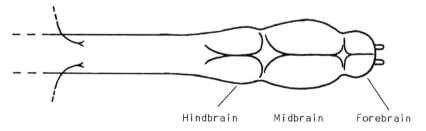

Hindbrain   Midbrain   Forebrain

Figure 7.2

Reptilian Brain

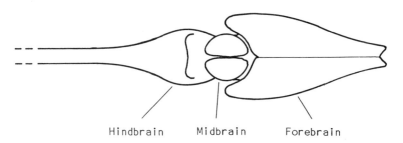

Hindbrain   Midbrain   Forebrain

Figure 7.3

Mammalian Brain

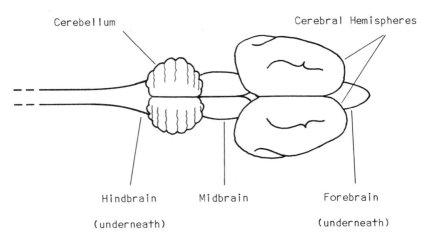

Cerebellum   Cerebral Hemispheres

Hindbrain   Midbrain   Forebrain

(underneath)   (underneath)

Figure 7.4

prey by means of excellent eyesight. A superior control system was essential if that ecological niche was to be occupied successfully.

The early mammalian brains display further articulation and specialization of the forebrain, and most important, two entirely new structures: the *cerebral hemispheres* growing out each side of the enlarged upper forebrain, and the *cerebellum* growing out of the back of the hindbrain (figure 7.4). The cerebral hemispheres contained a number of specialized areas, including the highest control for the initiation of behavior; and the cerebellum provided even better coordination of bodily motion in a world of objects in relative motion. The number of cells in the cerebral and cerebellar cortex (the thin surface at which cell bodies and intercellular connections are concentrated) is also strikingly larger than the number found in the more primtive cortex of reptiles. This cortical layer (the classical 'gray matter') is two to six times thicker in mammals.

In typical mammals these new structures, though prominent, are not large relative to the brain stem. In primates, however, they have become the dominant features of the brain, at least to the casual eye. And in humans, they have become enormous (figure 7.5). The old brain stem is barely visible underneath the umbrella of the cerebral hemispheres,

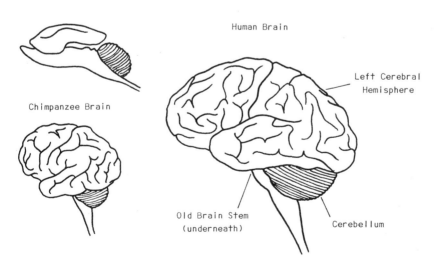

Side Views

Rat Brain (not to scale)

Human Brain

Left Cerebral
Hemisphere

Chimpanzee Brain

Old Brain Stem
(underneath)

Cerebellum

Figure 7.5

and the cerebellum is also markedly enlarged, compared to what other primates display. It is difficult to resist the suspicion that what distinguishes us from the other animals, to the extent that we are distinguished, is to be found in the large size and the unusual properties of the human cerebral and cerebellar hemispheres.

Suggested Readings

Bullock, T. H., Orkand, R., and Grinnell, A., *Introduction to Nervous Systems* (San Francisco: Freeman, 1977).

Sarnat, H. B., and Netsky, M. G., *Evolution of the Nervous System* (Oxford: Oxford University Press, 1974).

Dawkins, Richard, *The Selfish Gene* (Oxford: Oxford University Press, 1976).

2. Neurophysiology and Neural Organization

A. The Elements of the Network: Neurons

Structure and Function   The elongated impulse-carrying cells referred to earlier are called *neurons*. A typical multipolar neuron has the physical structure outlined in figure 7.6: a treelike structure of branching *dendrites* for input, and a single *axon* for output. (The axon is folded for diagrammatic reasons.) This structure reflects what appears to be the neuron's principal function: the processing of inputs from other cells. The axons of many other neurons make contact either with the dendrites of a given neuron, or with the cell body itself. These connections are called *synapses*, and they allow events in one cell to influence the activity of another (figure 7.7).

The influence is achieved in the following ways. When a depolarization pulse—called an *action potential* or *spike*—runs down the axon to its presynaptic ending(s), its arrival causes the terminal bulb to release a chemical called a *neurotransmitter* across the tiny synaptic cleft. Depending on the nature of the bulb's characteristic neurotransmitter, and on the nature of the chemical receptors that receive it on the opposite side of the cleft, the synapse is called either an *inhibitory* or an *excitatory* synapse.

In an inhibitory synapse, the synaptic transmission causes a slight *hyper*polarization or raising of the affected neuron's electric potential. This makes it less likely that the affected neuron will undergo a sudden depolarization and fire off its own spike along its own axon.

In an excitatory synapse, the synaptic transmission causes a slight *de*polarization of the affected neuron, inching its electric potential downward toward the critical minimum point where it suddenly col-

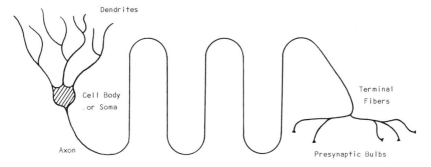

Figure 7.6

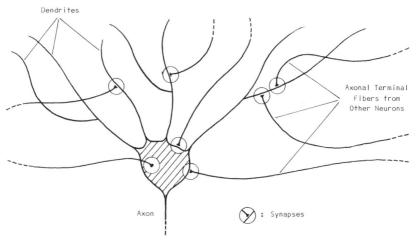

Dendrites

Axonal Terminal
Fibers from
Other Neurons

Axon   ⊗ : Synapses

Figure 7.7

lapses entirely, initiating its own axonal output spike. An excitatory synaptic event therefore makes it *more* likely that the affected neuron will fire.

Putting the two factors together, each neuron is the site of a competition between 'fire' and 'don't fire' inputs. Which side wins is determined by two things. First, the relative distribution of excitatory and inhibitory synapses matters greatly—their relative numbers, and perhaps their proximity to the main cell body. If one kind predominates, as often it does, then the deck is stacked, for that neuron, in favor of one response over the other. (In the very short term, these connections are a relatively stable feature of each neuron. But new connections do grow and old ones are lost, sometimes on a time scale of mere minutes or less; hence the functional properties of a neuron are themselves somewhat plastic.)

The second determinant of neuronal behavior is the sheer temporal frequency of inputs from synapses of each kind. If 2,000 inhibitory synapses are active only once per second, and 200 excitatory synapses are active a busy 50 times per second, then the excitatory influence will predominate and the neuron will fire. After repolarization, it will fire again, and again, with a significant frequency of its own.

It is well to keep in mind the relevant numbers here. A typical neuron soma will be almost buried under a layer of several hundred synapsing end bulbs, and its dendritic tree may enjoy synaptic connections with several thousands more. As well, neurons pump themselves back up to resting potential again in rather less than 1/100 second; hence they can sustain spiking frequencies of up to 100 hertz (= 100 spikes per second), or more. Evidently, a single neuron is an information processor of considerable capacity.

Inevitably, neurons are likened to the logic gates in the CPU of a digital computer. But the differences are as intriguing as the similarities. A single logic gate receives input from no more than two distinct sources; a neuron receives input from well in excess of a thousand. A logic gate emits outputs at a metronomic frequency, 10^6 hertz, for example; a neuron varies freely between 0 and 10^2 hertz. Logic-gate output is and must be temporally coordinated with that of all other gates; neuronal outputs are not thus coordinated. The function of a logic gate is the transformation of binary information (sets of ONs and OFFs) into further binary information; the function of a neuron, if we can even speak in the singular here, seems more plausibly to be the transformation of sets of spiking *frequencies* into further spiking *frequencies*. And last, the functional properties of a logic gate are fixed; those of a neuron are decidedly plastic, since the growth of new synaptic connections and the pruning or degeneration of old ones can change the input/output function of the cell. The dendritic branches can grow tiny spines in a matter of minutes, to effect new synaptic connections, and these changes are themselves induced, in part, by prior neuronal activity.

If neurons are information-processing devices, as almost certainly they are, their basic mode of operation is therefore very different from that displayed in the logic gates of a CPU. This is not to say that systems of the latter, suitably programmed, could not simulate the activities of the former. Presumably they could. But we need to know rather more about the plastic functional properties of neurons, and very much more about their myriad interconnections, before we can successfully simulate their collective activity.

Types of Neurons   An initial classification finds three kinds of neurons: *motor* neurons, *sensory* neurons, and a large variety of *interneurons* (that is, all the rest). Primary motor neurons are found almost exclusively in the spinal cord, and are defined as those neurons whose axons synapse directly onto a muscle cell. The axons of motor neurons are some of the longest in the nervous system, extending from deep within the spinal cord, out the *ventral roots* (see figure 7.1) between the spinal vertebrae, and on out the limbs to the most distant peripheral muscles. Motor neurons secure graded muscle contraction by two means: the spiking frequency of individual motor neurons, and the progressive recruitment of initially quiescent neurons that innervate the same muscle.

Sensory neurons come in greater variety, and are conventionally defined as those whose input stimulus is some dimension of the world outside the nervous system. For example, the rod and cone receptor cells of the retina are very tiny, with no axon to speak of, and no dendrites at all. They synapse immediately onto more typical neurons in a layer right next to them. Their job is solely to transform received light into synaptic events. The somatosensory cells, by contrast, are as long as the motor neurons. Their axons project from the skin and muscles into the spinal cord by way of the *dorsal roots* (see figure 7.1), and they find their first synapses deep in the spinal cord. Their job is to convey tactile, pain, and temperature information, and information about muscle extensions and contractions—the ever changing positions of the body and its limbs. Other sensory cells have their own idiosyncracies, dictated by the nature of the physical stimulus to which they respond.

The central interneurons also come in a great variety of shapes and sizes, though they all seem variations on the same theme: dendritic input and axonic output. Most, called multipolar cells, have many dendritic branches emerging directly from the cell body. Others, called bipolar cells, have only one dendritic thread emerging, which branches at a point some distance from the cell. Some, such as the Purkinje cells of the cerebellum, have extraordinarily extensive and bushy dendritic trees. Others enjoy only sparse dendritic extensions. The axons of many neurons project across the entire brain, synapsing at distant points. Others make merely local connections among extended concentrations of neurons whose axons project elsewhere.

These densely populated layers of heavily interconnected neuronal cell bodies are called *cortex*. The outer surface of each cerebral hemisphere is one large thin sheet of cortex, heavily folded upon itself like crumpled paper to maximize the total area achieved within the small volume of the skull. The brain's interneural connections are at their heaviest in this folded layer. The surface of the cerebellum is also cortex, and specialized cortical 'nuclei' are distributed throughout the brain stem. These show as gray areas in brain cross sections. The remaining white areas contain axonal projections from one cortical area to another. Which brings us to the matter of the brain's organization.

B. The Organization of the Network

Seeking organization in a network as complex as the human brain is a difficult business. Much structure has emerged, but as much or more remains shrouded in mystery. One can explore the large-scale structure of neuronal interconnections by using special stains that are taken up by a neuron and transported down its axon to the terminal synapses.

If we wish to know where the axons of a stained area project to, successive cross sections of the brain will reveal both the path those stained axons take through its relatively colorless volume, and the region of their ultimate terminus. This technique, applied to postmortem brains, has revealed the major interconnections between the various cortical areas of the brain, the 'superhighways' that involve many thousands of axons strung together. Knowing their locations does not always reveal their functions, however, and the smaller neuronal highways and byways constitute a horizon of ever shrinking detail that defies attempts at complete summary.

With microscopes, thin sections, and a variety of further staining techniques, the microarchitecture of the brain begins to emerge. Cerebral cortex reveals six distinct layers, distinguished by the density of the neuron populations within them, and by the type of neurons they contain. Interneuronal communication is extensive, both within layers and across them. The details are complex and obscure, and the point of this particular arrangement remains mysterious, but we cling to what order we discover, and try to use it to find more. As it happens, this six-layered cytoarchitecture is not entirely uniform through the cerebral cortex: the thickness or density of certain layers is diminished or exaggerated in certain areas of the cortical surface. Tracing areas of identical architecture, and noting their boundaries, has led us to identify about fifty distinct cortical areas, known as *Brodmann's areas* after their discoverer.

Are these areas of any further significance? Many of them are, both in their functional properties and in their more distant connections. A few salient cases will now be outlined.

Sensory Projections within the Brain   As mentioned earlier, the primary somatosensory neurons enter the spinal cord via the dorsal roots, and find their first synaptic connections with neurons in the cord. Those neurons conduct the information up the spinal cord all the way to the thalamus in the forebrain, where they synapse onto neurons in an area called the ventral thalamic nucleus. These neurons project in turn into the cerebral hemispheres, and into a cortical area neatly defined by three connecting Brodmann's areas. This overall area is now known as the *somatosensory cortex*. Damage to various parts of it produces a permanent loss of tactile and proprioceptive awareness of various parts of the body. Moreover, subtle electrical stimulation of neurons in this area produces in the subject vivid tactile sensations 'located' in specific parts of the body. (Brain surgery to correct threats to this area has provided the occasional opportunity for such probing, and since subjects can be wholly conscious during brain surgery, they can report the effects of such stimulations.)

In fact, the somatosensory cortex constitutes what is called a *topographic map* of the body, since the spatial arrangement of anatomically specific neurons is a projection of the anatomical areas themselves. Each hemisphere represents the opposite one-half of the body. The cross section of one hemisphere in figure 7.8 illustrates this point. The distorted creature represents the areas of the cortex devoted to the body part next to it, and the variations in size represent the relative numbers of cortical cells devoted to that part. This diagrammatic creature is called "the somatosensory homunculus".

The organization and function of the visual system also makes contact with the architecture of the cerebral cortex. Right next to the primary rods and cones of the retina is an interconnected layer of small neurons that performs some initial processing before synapsing onto the long ganglion cells. These cluster together in a thick bundle and exit the back of the retina as the optic nerve. The optic nerve projects to a cortical nucleus (= a local concentration of interconnected cell bodies) at the rear of the thalamus called the *lateral geniculate body*. The cells here also constitute a topographic map of the retina, though it is metrically distorted in that the fovea, the physical and functional center of the retina, is very heavily represented.

Cells in the lateral geniculate then project to several of Brodmann's

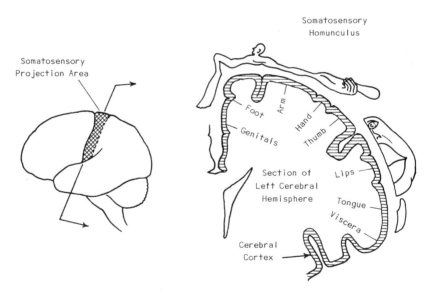

Figure 7.8

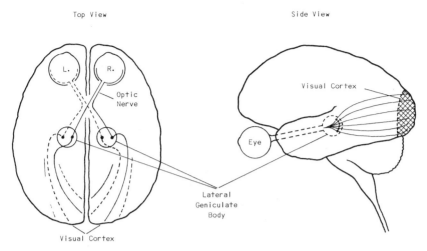

Top View   Side View

Visual Cortex

Optic
Nerve

Eye

Lateral
Geniculate
Body

Visual Cortex

Figure 7.9

areas on the rearmost surface of the cerebral hemispheres: to the striate
cortex and thence to the peristriate cortex (figure 7.9). These collected
areas are called the *visual cortex*, and still constitute a topographic
projection of the retina, each hemisphere representing one-half of the
retinal surface. But rather more is going on in the visual cortex, and
in its precortical processing, than occurs in the somatosensory system,
and the visual cortex represents rather more than just areas of retinal
stimulation. Subpopulations of visual neurons turn out to be specialized,
in their responses, to highly specific features of the visual information.
A cell early in the hierarchy is sensitive only to brightness *differences*
within its receptive field (= the retinal area to which it is sensitive).
But a higher cell to which these early cells project may be sensitive
only to lines or edges of a particular *orientation* within its receptive
field. Cells higher still are sensitive only to lines or edges *moving* in a
particular direction. And so on. The impression of a cumulative information-processing system is impossible to escape.

  Further microstructures promise to explicate the features of binocular
vision—in particular, the sophisticated *stereopsis* or three-dimensional
vision possessed by humans. Stereopsis requires the systematic comparison of the images from each eye. Close examination reveals the
existence of interleaved *ocular dominance columns* in the visual cortex.
A column is a narrow cluster of cells organized vertically through the
six layers of the cortex, and each has a small receptive field in the
retina. Such columns are eye-specific, and their interleaving means that
corresponding left and right receptive fields are represented by phys-

ically adjacent columns in the cortex. Comparison of information can thus take place, and further cells have been discovered that are indeed sensitive to binocular disparities between those fields. Such cells are responding to information about the relative distances of the objects in one's visual environment. These discoveries open promising lines of research, and the visual cortex currently commands a great deal of interest.

Motor Projections Outward   Just in front of the somatosensory cortex, on the other side of a largish cleft, is another of Brodmann's areas now known as the *motor cortex*. This is also a clear topographic map, this time of the body's muscle systems. Artificial stimulation of motor cortical neurons produces movement in the corresponding muscles. A 'motor homunculus' is displayed in figure 7.10.

This is only the beginning of the functional story, of course, since motor control is a matter of well-orchestrated *sequences* of muscle contractions—sequences, moreover, that cohere with the body's perceived environment. Accordingly, the motor cortex has axonal projections, not just to the cord and thence to the body's muscles, but to the cerebellum and the basal ganglia, and it receives reciprocal projections from both, primarily through the thalamus, which we already know to be a source of sensory information. The motor cortex is therefore a highly integrated part of general brain activity, and though some of

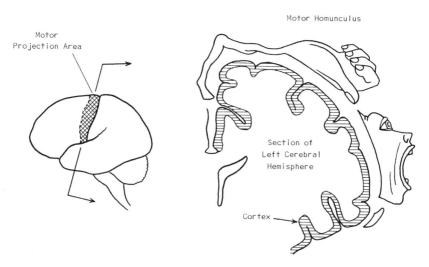

Figure 7.10

its output goes more or less directly to the cord—to provide independent control of fine finger movements, for example—much of it goes through intricate processing in the cerebellum and lower brain stem before entering the spinal cord.

We must think of the brain's output here as a sort of high-level 'fine tuning' of motor capacities more basic still, since the neural organization of the spinal cord itself is sufficient to produce locomotion in most vertebrates. A familiar example is the headless chicken whose body runs around aimlessly for several seconds after slaughter. Even small mammals whose brains have been substantially removed will display locomotor activity upon suitable stimulation of the cord. We have here a reflection of just how very *old* the capacity for vertebrate locomotion is; it was first perfected when primitive vertebrates enjoyed little more than a spinal cord. The progressive additions that survived did so because they added some useful fine tuning of, or intelligent guidance to, that initial capacity. The motor cortex is merely one of the later and higher centers in an extensive hierarchy of motor controls. These extend from the simple reflex arcs—such as will withdraw a hand from a hot stove—up to the highest centers, which formulate abstract, long-term plans of action.

Internal Organization   The brain monitors the extra-nervous world, through the primary sensory neurons; but in the process it also monitors many aspects of its own operations. And the brain exerts control over the extra-nervous world; but it also exerts control over many aspects of its own operations. The internal projections among parts of the brain are rich and extensive, and they are critical to its functioning. A good example is the existence of 'descending control' mechanisms. In our earlier discussion of the visual system I did not mention that the visual cortex also sends projections *back* to the lateral geniculate body in the thalamus, where the optic nerve terminates. What this means is that, depending on what the visual cortex is getting from the lateral geniculate, it can exert an influence on the latter to *change* what is being sent, perhaps to highlight certain features of the input, or to suppress others. We have here the elements of some plasticity in the brain's processing activities, the capacity for directing attention and focusing resources. Descending control pathways are especially prominent in the visual system and in the auditory system, which must process speech, but they are common throughout the brain.

Between the sensory areas of the cortex here discussed, and other sensory areas similarly identified, there remains a great deal of highly active brain. The large so-called "association areas", between the various types of sensory cortex, are not well understood, and neither are the large frontal areas of the cerebral hemispheres, though it is plain from cases of brain damage that these latter are impicated in emotion, drive, and the capacity for planned action.

There is a hypothesis that makes general sense of these areas, of their function and of their axonal connections with other areas. Consider figure 7.11. The cross-hatched areas are the areas of *primary* sensory cortex: somatosensory, auditory, and visual. The vertically striped areas are *secondary* sensory cortex. Cells in the primary cortex project to cells in the secondary cortex, for all three sensory modalities, and these secondary cells are responsive to more complex and abstract features of the sensory input than are the cells in the primary cortex. Secondary cortex, in turn, projects into the unshaded areas, called *tertiary* or *association* cortex. Cells in the association cortex are responsive to still more abstract features of the original sensory inputs, but here we find a mixture of cells, some responsive to visual input, some to auditory input, some to tactile input, and some to combinations of all three. It would appear that the brain's most abstract and integrated analysis of the sensory environment takes place in the association cortex between the several sensory areas.

From this rear or 'sensory' half of the brain, information can make its way by a variety of underlying pathways in the midbrain to the frontal or 'motor' half of the brain, into what we may call the tertiary

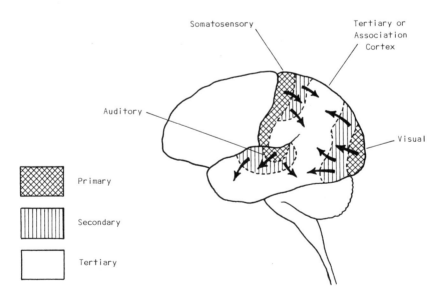

Figure 7.11

motor areas. This is the unshaded frontal area in figure 7.12. This area appears responsible for the formation of our most general plans and intentions. Cells here project into the secondary motor cortex, which appears to be the locus of more specifically conceived plans and sequences of behavior. This area projects finally to the primary motor cortex, which is responsible for highly specific motions of the various parts of the body.

This hypothesis is consistent with the neuroarchitecture of the brain, with its overall capacities as a sensorily guided control of bodily behavior, and with detailed studies of the specific cognitive deficits produced by lesions at various sites in the brain. Damage to the extreme frontal lobe, for example, leaves the victim unable to conceive of, or to distinguish in a caring fashion between, alternative possible futures beyond the most immediate and simple matters.

The preceding sketch of the global organization of the brain represents the classical view, but the reader should be warned that it presents a provisional and oversimplified picture. Recent studies indicate that distinct topographic maps of the retina are scattered throughout the cortical surface, and enjoy distinct projections from the lateral geniculate, or from elsewhere in the thalamus. The hierachical system of topographic maps discussed earlier, which culminates in the 'secondary visual cortex' at the rear of the brain, is thus only one of several parallel systems, each processing different aspects of visual input. The 'classical' system

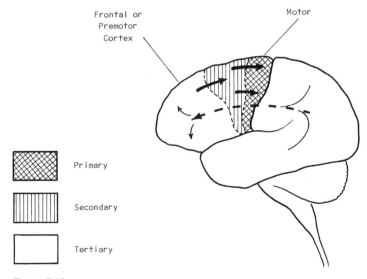

Figure 7.12

for vision may be the dominant one, but it has company, and all of these systems interact. Similar complexities attend the 'somatosensory cortex', which emerges as only one of several parallel systems processing different types of somatosensory information: light touch, deep pressure, limb position, pain, temperature, and so forth. Sorting out the functional differences between these distinct maps and tracing their functional interconnections is a job that has only begun. As that information does emerge, our appreciation of the intricate and occasionally unsuspected achievements of our perceptual system must grow in equal measure.

One further area of intrigue is worthy of mention, not because it is large, but because it is the ultimate target of a hierarchy of projections from very large and varied areas of the cerebral cortex. The smallish *hippocampus* is at the back end of the limbic system, a forebrain structure just underneath the great cerebral hemispheres. If we trace the inputs to the hippocampus back to their origins, against the flow of incoming information, we fairly quickly implicate the entire cerebral cortex. Damage to the hippocampus, it emerges, blocks the transfer of information from short-term into long-term memory. Victims of such damage live in a nightmare world of no memories reaching longer than a few minutes into the past, save those original memories, of those ever more distant events, entrenched before the injury occurred.

It is natural to think of the brain as something which is interposed between the peripheral sensory nerves and the peripheral motor nerves, something controlled by the former and in control of the latter. From an evolutionary perspective, this makes sense, at least in the early stages. But with the brain at the level of articulation and self-modulation found in humans, a certain autonomy has crept into the picture. Our behavior is governed as much by our past learning, and by our plans for the long-term future, as by our current perceptions. And through self-directed learning, the long-term development of the brain's internal organization is to some extent under the control of the brain itself. We do not by this means escape the animal kingdom, but we are become its most creative and unpredictable members.

Suggested Readings

Churchland, Patricia, *Neurophilosophy* (Cambridge, MA: MIT Press, 1986).

Hubel, D. H., and Wiesel, T. N., "Brain Mechanisms of Vision," *Scientific American*, vol. 241, no. 3 (September 1979): a special issue devoted to the various brain sciences.

Bullock, T. H., Orkand, R., and Grinnell, A., *Introduction to Nervous Systems* (San Francisco: Freeman, 1977).

Kandel, E. R., and Schwartz, J. H., *Principles of Neural Science* (New York: Elsevier/North-Holland, 1981).

Kandel, E. R., *The Cellular Basis of Behavior* (San Francisco: Freeman, 1976).

Shepherd, G. M., *Neurobiology* (New York: Oxford University Press, 1983).

3. *Neuropsychology*

Neuropsychology is the discipline that attempts to understand and explain psychological phenomena in terms of the neurochemical, neurophysiological, and neurofunctional activities of the brain. We have already seen some tentative but intriguing neuropsychological results in the preceding section: how the hierarchical structure of the visual system permits us to discriminate selected features from a scene, how interleaved retinal representations on the cortical surface make stereo vision possible, and how the overall organization of the cortex makes it possible for highly processed sensory information to guide the formation and execution of general plans of action.

Unfortunately, the greater portion of the data traditionally available to neuropsychology derives from cases of brain damage, degeneration, and disequilibrium. What we understand best is the neural basis of *abnormal* psychology. Brain tissue can be physically disrupted by invasive objects; it can be crushed by growing tumors or fluid pressure; it can starve and atrophy from localized loss of blood supply; or it can be selectively destroyed by disease or degeneration. Depending on the specific *location*, within the brain, of the lesion produced by any of these means, very specific losses in the victim's psychological capacities typically result.

Such losses may be minor, as with an inability to identify perceived colors (lesions to the connections between the secondary visual cortex and the secondary auditory cortex of the left hemisphere). Or they may be serious, as with the permanent inability to recognize faces, even those of family members (lesions in the association cortex of the right hemisphere). And they can be devastating, as with the total and permanent loss of speech comprehension (lesions to the secondary auditory cortex of the left hemisphere), or the inability to lay down new memories (bilateral damage to the hippocampus).

Using postmortem examination, and other diagnostic techniques, neurologists and neuropsychologists can find the neural correlates of these and hundreds of other losses in cognitive and behavioral function. By this means we can slowly piece together an overall *functional map* of the brain. We can come to appreciate the functional specializations and the functional organization of the brain in a *normal* human. This information, in conjunction with a detailed understanding of the neuroarchitecture and microactivity of the relevant areas, can lead to a real understanding of how our cognitive capacities are actually produced. Recall our glimpse into feature extraction and stereopsis in the visual system. Once we know where to look for them, we can start to find specific neural structures that account for the specific features of the cognitive capacity at issue. Overall, there is cause for much optimism here, even though our ignorance still dwarfs our understanding.

The functional sleuthing just described requires caution in two respects. First, the simple correlation of a lesion in area x with the loss of some cognitive function F does not mean that area x has the function F. It means only that some part of area x is typically involved in some way in the execution of F. The key neural structures that sustain F may be located elsewhere, or they may not be localized at all, being distributed over large areas of the brain.

Second, we must not expect that the functional losses and functional localizations that we do find will always correspond neatly with cognitive functions represented in our common-sense psychological vocabulary. Sometimes the deficit is difficult to describe, as when it involves a global change in the victim's personality, and sometimes its description is difficult to credit. For example, some lesions produce a complete loss of awareness, both perceptual and practical, of the *left half* of the victim's universe, including the victim's own body (hemineglect). A victim will typically dress only the right side of his body, and even deny ownership of his own left arm. Other lesions leave the victim able to write lucid, readable prose, but *una*ble to read and understand what she or anyone else has written, even though her vision is wholly normal (alexia without agraphia). Further lesions leave the victim 'blind', in the sense that his visual field has disappeared and he insists that he cannot see; and yet he can 'guess' where a light is placed in front of him with an accuracy approaching 100 percent (blind-sight). Still other lesions leave the victim genuinely and utterly blind, but the victim perversely insists that she *can* see perfectly, as she stumbles about the room confabulating excuses for her clumsy behavior (blindness denial).

These cases are surprising and confusing, relative to the familiar conceptions of folk psychology. How could one possibly be blind and not know it? See with no visual field? Write freely but not read a word? Or sincerely deny ownership of arms and legs attached to oneself? These cases violate entrenched expectations. But we cannot expect that folk psychology represents anything more than one stage in the historical development of our self-understanding, a stage the neurosciences may help us to transcend.

Beneath the level of structural damage to our neural machinery, there is the level of chemical activity and chemical abnormalities. The reader will recall that transmission across the synaptic junction is a critical element in all neural activity, and that such transmission is chemical in nature. Upon receipt of an impulse or spike, the axonal end bulb releases a chemical called a *neurotransmitter* that swiftly diffuses across the synaptic cleft to interact with chemical receptors on the far side.

This interaction leads to the breakdown of the neurotransmitter chemical, and the breakdown products are eventually taken up again by the end bulb for resynthesis and reuse.

Evidently, anything that frustrates, or exaggerates, these chemical activities will have a profound effect on neural commmunication and on collective neural activity. This is precisely how the many psychoactive drugs work their effects. The various types of neurons make use of distinct neurotransmitters, and different drugs have different effects on their activity, so there is room here for a wide variety of effects, both chemical and psychological. A drug may block the synthesis of a specific neurotransmitter; or bind to its receptor sites, thus blocking its effects; or block the uptake of its breakdown products, thus slowing its resynthesis. On the other hand, a drug may enhance synthesis, increase receptor sites, or accelerate the uptake of breakdown products. Alcohol, for example, is an antagonist to the action of noradrenaline, an important neurotransmitter, whereas the amphetamines enhance its activity, producing the very opposite psychological effect.

Most important, extreme doses of certain of the psychoactive drugs produce symptoms that closely resemble those of the major forms of mental illness—depression, mania, and schizophrenia. This suggests the hypothesis that these illnesses, as they occur naturally, involve the same neurochemical abnormality as is artificially produced by these drugs. Such hypotheses are of much more than purely theoretical interest because if they are true, then the naturally occurring illness may well be correctable or controllable by a drug with an exactly opposite neurochemical effect. And thus it seems to be, though the situation is complex and the details are confusing. *Imipramine* controls depression, *lithium* controls mania, and *chlorpromazine* controls schizophrenia. Imperfectly, it must be said, but the qualified success of these drugs lends strong support to the view that the victims of mental illness are the victims primarily of sheer chemical circumstance, whose origins are more metabolic and biological than they are social or psychological. If so, this fact is important, since better than 2 percent of the human population has a significant encounter with one of these conditions at some point in their lives. If we can discover the nature and origins of the complex chemical imbalances that underlie the major forms of mental illness, we may be able to cure them outright or even prevent their occurrence entirely.

Suggested Readings

Kolb, B., and Whishaw, I. Q., *Fundamentals of Human Neuropsychology* (San Francisco: Freeman, 1980).

Gardner, H., *The Shattered Mind* (New York: Knopf, 1975).

4. Cognitive Neurobiology

As its name implies, cognitive neurobiology is an interdisciplinary area of research whose concern is to understand the specifically cognitive activities displayed by living creatures. It has begun to flower in recent years, for three reasons.

First, there has been a steady improvement in the *technologies* that allow us to explore the microstructure of the brain and to monitor our ongoing neural activities. Modern electron microscopes give us an unparalleled access to the details of brain microstructure, and various nuclear technologies allow us to image the internal structure and neural activity of living brains without invading or disrupting them at all. Second, research has benefited from the appearance of some provocative general *theories* about the function of large-scale neural networks. These theories give a direction and purpose to our experimental efforts; they help tell us what are the useful questions to ask of Nature. And third, modern *computers* have made it possible for us to explore, in an efficient and revealing way, the functional properties of the highly intricate structures that recent theories ascribe to our brains. For we can model such structures within a computer and then let the computer tell us how they will behave under various circumstances. We can then test these predictions against the behavior of real brains in comparable circumstances.

In this section we will take a brief look at two of the central questions of cognitive neurobiology. How does the brain *represent* the world? And how does the brain perform *computations* over those representations? Let us take the first question first, and let us begin with some entirely familiar phenomena.

How does the brain represent the color of a sunset? The smell of a rose? The taste of a peach? Or the face of a loved one? There is a simple technique for representing, or *coding*, external features that is surprisingly effective, and can be used in all of the cases mentioned, despite their diversity. To see how it works, consider the case of taste.

Sensory Coding: Taste   On one's tongue, there are four distinct kinds of receptor cells. Cells of each kind respond in their own peculiar way to any given substance that makes contact with them. A peach, for example, might have a substantial effect on one of the four kinds of cells, a minimal effect on the second kind, and some intermediate levels of effect on the third and fourth kinds. Taken together, this exact pattern of relative stimulations constitutes a sort of neural 'fingerprint' that is uniquely characteristic of peaches.

If we name the four kinds of cells, a, b, c, and d, respectively, then we can describe exactly what that special fingerprint is, by specifying the four levels of neural stimulation that contact with a peach produces. If we use the letter S, with a subscript, to represent each of the various levels of stimulation, then the following is what we want: $\langle S_a,$ $S_b, S_c, S_d \rangle$. This is called a *sensory coding vector* (a vector is just a list of numbers, or a set of magnitudes). The important point is that there is evidently a *unique* coding vector for every humanly possible taste. Which is to say, any humanly possible taste sensation is just a pattern of stimulation levels across the four kinds of sensory cells. Or better, it is a pattern of spiking frequencies across the four neural channels that convey news of these activity levels away from the mouth and to the rest of the brain.

We can graphically display any given taste by means of an appropriate point in a 'taste-space', a space with four axes, one each for the stimulation level in each of the four kinds of sensory taste cell. Figure 7.13 depicts a space in which the positions of various tastes are coded. (In this diagram, one of the four axes has been suppressed, since it is

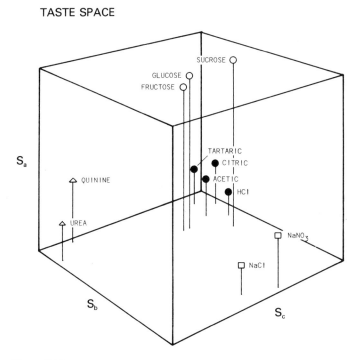

Figure 7.13

hard to draw a 4-D space on a 2-D page.) What is interesting is that subjectively similar tastes turn out to have very similar coding vectors. Or what is the same thing, their points in taste-space are very close together. You will notice that various types of 'sweet' taste all get coded in the upper regions of the space, while sundry 'tart' tastes appear in the lower center. Various 'bitter' tastes appear at the lower left, and 'salty' tastes reside in the region to the lower right. The other points in that space represent all of the other taste sensations it is possible for humans to have. Here there is definite encouragement for the identity theorist's suggestion (chapter 2, section 3) that any given sensation is simply identical with a set of spiking frequencies in the appropriate sensory pathway.

Sensory Coding: Color   A somewhat similar story appears to hold for color. There are three distinct types of color-sensitive cells or *cones* in the human retina, each type being sensitive to a distinct wavelength of light: short, medium, and long waves respectively. Color vision is a complex matter, and my brief sketch here is badly oversimplified, but a central part of the story appears to be the *pattern* of activity levels produced across the three distinct types of cones. Here the sensory coding vector appears to have three elements, rather than four: $\langle S_{short}, S_{medium}, S_{long} \rangle$. But again, similarities in color turn out to be reflected in the similarities of their coding vectors, or what is the same, by the closeness of their points in a 3-D 'color-sensation space' (figure 7.14). Also, the intuitive idea that orange is somehow 'between' red and yellow gets a straightforward expression: if color sensations are represented in this way, the sensation of orange is *literally* between the other two kinds of sensation. And so with all the other 'betweenness' relations in the domain of color.

Finally it is worth noting that this view of sensory coding also accounts for the several varieties of color-blindness. Victims of this minor disorder are missing one (or more) of the three types of cones. Which means that their 'color space' will have only two (or fewer) dimensions, rather than three. Which means that their ability to discriminate colors will be reduced in predictable ways.

Sensory Coding: Smell   The olfactory system appears to involve six or seven, and perhaps more, distinct kinds of receptors. This suggests that smells are coded by a vector of spiking frequencies with at least six or seven different elements. This allows for a great many distinct combinations of frequencies, and thus for a great many distinct smells. Let us suppose that

COLOR QUALIA SPACE

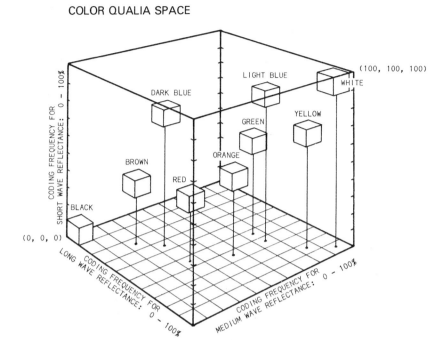

Figure 7.14

a bloodhound, for example, has seven kinds of olfactory receptors and can distinguish thirty different levels of stimulation within each type. On these assumptions, we must credit the bloodhound with an overall 'smell space' of $30 \times 30 \times 30 \times 30 \times 30 \times 30 \times 30$ ($= 30^7$ or 22 *billion*) discriminable positions! No wonder dogs can distinguish any one person from among millions, by smell alone.

All of this must provide encouragement for the identity theorists, who claim that our sensations are simply identical with, say, a set of stimulation levels (spiking frequencies) in the appropriate sensory pathways. For as the preceding sections show, neuroscience is success-fully reconstructing, in a systematic and revealing way, the various fea-tures of, and the relations between, our subjective sensory qualia. This is the same pattern that, during the nineteenth century, motivated the scientific claim that light is simply identical with electromagnetic waves of a certain frequency. For within the theory of electricity and magnetism, we could systematically reconstruct all of the familiar fea-tures of light.

Sensory Coding: Faces   Among humans, it is *faces* that get distinguished with great skill, and a recent theory says that faces are also handled by a vector-coding strategy. For each of the various elements of a human face to which we are perceptually sensitive—nose length, width of mouth, distance between eyes, squareness of jaw, etc., etc.—suppose there is a pathway whose level of stimulation corresponds to the degree to which the perceived face displays that element. A particular face, therefore, will be coded by a unique vector of stimulations, a vector whose elements correspond to the visible elements of the face perceived.

If we guess that there are perhaps ten different facial features to which a mature human is automatically sensitive, and if we suppose that we can distinguish at least five different levels within each feature, then we must credit humans with a 'facial space' of at least 5^{10} (about 10 million) discriminable positions. Small wonder we can distinguish any person from among millions, by sight alone.

The faces of close relatives, of course, will be coded by vectors with many of the same or similar elements. By contrast, people bearing no resemblance to each other will be coded by quite disparate vectors. A person with a supremely average face will be coded by a vector where all of the elements are in the middle of the relevant range of variation. And someone with a highly distinctive face will be coded by a vector that has one or more elements at an extreme value. Interestingly, the parietal lobe of the right cerebral cortex in humans, a large area responsible for spatial matters in general, has a small part whose destruction produces an inability to recognize human faces. Here, we may postulate, are human faces coded.

Sensory Coding: The   The virtues of vector coding are
Motor System   especially apparent when we consider the problem of representing a very complex system, such as the simultaneous position of all of the thousands of muscles in one's body. You have a constant and continuously updated sense of the overall posture or configuration of your body in space. And a good thing, too. To be able to effect any useful movements at all, you must know where your limbs are starting from. This goes for simple things like walking, just as much as for complex things like ballet or basketball.

This sense of one's bodily configuration is called *proprioception*, and it is possible because each and every muscle in the body has its own nerve fiber constantly sending information back to the brain, information about the contraction or extension of that muscle. With so many muscles, the total coding vector in the brain will plainly have, not three elements, or ten, but something over a thousand elements! But that is no problem for the brain: it has *billions* of fibers with which to do the job.

Output Coding

While we are talking about the motor system, you might notice that vector coding can be just as useful for directing motor *output* as it is for coding sensory input. When a person is engaged in any physical activity at all, the brain is sending a cascade of distinct messages to every muscle in the body. But those messages must be well organized if the body is to do anything coherent: every muscle must assume just the right degree of contraction or extension if they are to make the body assume the position desired.

How can the brain orchestrate all of this? By means of a *motor vector:* a set of simultaneous activity levels in all of the motor neurons, neurons that convey messages from the brain to the body's muscles. A complex movement is a sequence of bodily positions, and so for these the brain must issue not one, but a sequence of motor vectors. Typically, these output vectors are sent down the tens of thousands of long axons in the spinal cord and then out along the motor neurons to the muscles themselves. Here each element of the large vector is realized as a stimulation level in the neuron that makes contact with the appropriate muscle. The muscle responds to that one element of the vector, contracting or relaxing as the level of simulation decrees. Collectively, and if the motor vectors are well constituted, these individual stimulations make the entire body move with coherence and grace.

Neural Computing

As we have seen, stimulation vectors are a beautifully effective means of representing things as various as tastes, faces, and complex limb positions. Equally important, it turns out that they are also part of a very elegant solution to the problem of high-speed computing. If the brain uses vectors to code various sensory inputs, and also various motor outputs, then it must somewhere be performing computations so that the inputs are in some way *guiding* or *producing* the outputs. In short, it needs some arrangement to transform its various sensory input vectors into appropriate motor output vectors.

As it happens, large segments of the brain have a microstructure that seems ideally suited to performing transformations of precisely this kind. Consider, for example, the schematic arrangement of axons, dendrites, and synapses in figure 7.15. Here the input vector, $\langle a, b, c, d \rangle$,

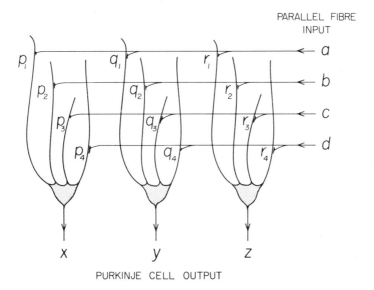

PARALLEL FIBRE
INPUT

PURKINJE CELL OUTPUT

Figure 7.15

is realized in the four horizontal input axons. Each axon is conducting
an incoming train of spikes with a certain frequency. And as you can
see, each axon makes three synaptic connections, one for each of the
three vertical cells. (These are called *Purkinje cells*, after their discoverer.) Altogether, that makes $4 \times 3 = 12$ synapses.

But these synaptic connections are not all identical. As the diagram
displays, some are large. Others are small. The letters p_i, q_j, and r_k represent their magnitude. To calculate the amount of excitation each connection induces in its receiving cell, just multiply the size of the
connection times the spiking frequency in the incoming axon. The *total*
excitation in the receiving Purkinje cell is then just the sum of those
four synaptic effects.

The Purkinje cell emits a train of spikes down its own output axon,
a train whose frequency is a function of the total excitation that the
various inputs have produced in that cell. Since all three of the Purkinje cells do this, the output of the system is obviously another vector,
a vector with three elements. Plainly, our little system will transform any
4-D input vector into a quite different 3-D output vector.

What determines the nature of the overall transformation is of course
the distribution of *sizes* among the various synaptic connections. These
connection strengths are usually called *weights*. If we specify the distribution of the synaptic weights in a system of this sort, we have spec-

ified the character of the transformation it will perform on any incoming vector.

The Cerebellum   The vector-transforming system of figure 7.15 is just a schematic sketch, highly simplified for purposes of illustration. But the same type of cellular organization appears in the cerebellum of all creatures, though on a much larger scale. Figure 7.16 depicts a tiny section of the cerebellar cortex, and you can see that the many Mossy-fiber inputs conduct their various spiking frequencies through the granule cells and out to the *parallel fibers*, each one of which makes multiple synaptic connections with the bushy dendritic trees of many different Purkinje cells. Each Purkinje cell sums the activity thus induced in it and emits a train of spikes down its own axon as output. The assembled activity levels in the entire set of Purkinje axons constitutes the cerebellum's output vector.

Figure 7.16 is also a simplification, because in a real cerebellum there are millions of parallel fibers, many hundreds of thousands of Purkinje

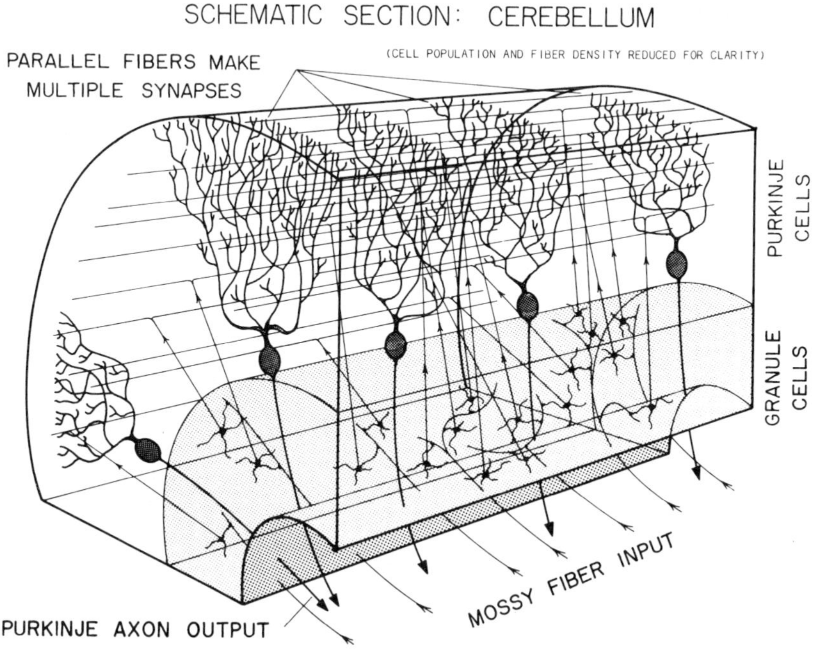

SCHEMATIC SECTION: CEREBELLUM

Figure 7.16

cells, and billions of synaptic connections. On the face of it then, the input vector has millions of elements, and the output vector has hundreds of thousands, although there is likely to be a good deal of redundancy, in the sense that each element of the true vector may be multiply coded. In any case, we here have coding vectors that are easily large enough to do the job of coordinating the body's muscle system. And that is precisely what the cerebellum appears to do. The cerebellum's major output goes down the spinal cord and out to the muscles. And if the cerebellum is severely damaged or lost, the victim's voluntary movements become jerky, badly aimed, and uncoordinated.

There are three important points to notice about a 'computing' system of the kind displayed in the cerebellum. First, it is highly resistant to minor damage and scattered cell death. Since it is made up of billions of synaptic connections, each of which contributes only a tiny bit to the overall transformation of vectors, the loss of a few thousand connections here and there will change the network's global behavior hardly at all. It can even lose millions of connections, so long as they are scattered randomly throughout the network, as happens with the gradual death of cells in the natural course of aging. The quality of the cerebellum's computation will therefore slowly *degrade*, rather than fall off suddenly.

Second, a massively parallel system of this kind will perform its vector-to-vector transformations in an instant. Because each synapse performs its own 'calculation' more or less simultaneously with every other synapse, the billion or so calculations required to produce the output vector are done all at once, rather than one after the other. The output vector will be on its way to the muscles less than ten milliseconds (1/100th of a second) after the input vector hits the network. Even though synapses are much slower than CPUs, and even though the axonal propagation of spikes is vastly slower than electrical propagation, the cerebellum performs this global calculation hundreds of times faster than the very fastest serial computer. Its massive parallelism is what makes the difference.

Third, such networks are functionally modifiable. In technical parlance, they are *plastic*. They can change their transformational properties simply by changing some or all of their synaptic weights. This is an important fact, since it must be possible for the system to learn to produce coordinated motion in the first place, and then to continually relearn, as the size and mass of the limbs slowly changes with age. How such learning might occur we shall discuss presently.

In summary, neural networks of this sort are computationally powerful, damage-resistant, fast, and modifiable. Nor do their virtues end here, as we are about to see in the next section.

Suggested Readings

Llinas, R., "The Cortex of the Cerebellum," *Scientific American*, 232, no. 1 (1975).

Bartoshuk, L. M., "Gustatory System," in *Handbook of Behavioral Neurobiology, Vol. I, Sensory Integration*, R. B. Masterton, ed. (New York: Plenum, 1978).

Pfaff, D. W., *Taste, Olfaction, and the Central Nervous System* (New York: Rockefeller University Press, 1985).

Land, E., "The Retinex Theory of Color Vision," *Scientific American*, 237, no. 6 (Dec., 1977).

Hardin, C. L., *Color for Philosophers* (Indianapolis: Hackett, 1987).

Dewdney, A. K., "A Whimsical Tour of Face Space," in the Computer Recreations section of *Scientific American*, vol. 255 (Oct., 1986).

Pellionisz, A., and Llinas, R., "Tensor Network Theory of the Metaorganization of Functional Geometries in the Central Nervous System," *Neuroscience*, vol. 19 (1986).

Churchland, P. M., "Some Reductive Strategies in Cognitive Neurobiology," *Mind*, vol. 95, no. 379 (1986).

Churchland, P. S., *Neurophilosophy* (Cambridge, MA: The MIT Press, 1986).

5. AI Again: Parallel Distributed Processing

In the late 50s, very early in the history of AI, there was considerable interest in artificial 'neural networks', that is, in hardware systems modelled on the biological brain. Despite their initial appeal, these first-generation networks were shown to have serious limitations, and they were quickly eclipsed by the techniques of 'program-writing' AI. These latter have since proved to have severe limitations of their own, as we saw at the end of chapter 6, and recent years have seen a rebirth of interest in the earlier approach. Early limitations have been transcended, and artificial neural networks are finally beginning to display their real potential.

Artificial Neural Networks: Their Structure Consider a network composed of simple, neuron-like units, connected in the fashion displayed in figure 7.17. The bottom units may be thought of as sensory units, as they are stimulated by the environment outside the system. Each of these bottom units emits an output through its own 'axon', an output whose strength is a function of the unit's level of stimulation. The axon divides into a number of terminal

A SIMPLE NETWORK

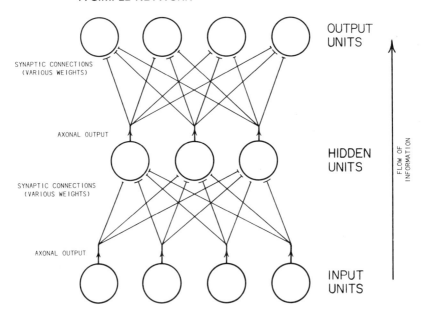

Figure 7.17

branches, and a copy of that output signal is conveyed to each and every unit at the second level. These are called the *hidden units*, and the bottom units make a variety of 'synaptic connections' with each of them. Each connection has a certain strength or *weight*, as it is commonly called.

You can see already that the bottom half of the system is just another vector-to-vector transformer, much like the neural matrices discussed in the previous section. If we stimulate the bottom units, the set of activity levels we induce (the input vector) will be conveyed upward toward the hidden units. On the way, it gets transformed by various influences: by the output function of the bottom cells, by whatever pattern of weights resides in the many synapses, and by the summing activity within each of the hidden units. The result is a set or pattern of stimulation levels across the hidden units: another vector.

That stimulation vector in the hidden units serves in turn as the input vector to the top half of the system. The axons from the hidden units make synaptic connections, of various weights, with the units at the topmost level. These are the output units, and the overall set of stimulation levels finally induced in them is what constitutes the output vector. The upper half of the network is thus just another vector-to-vector transformer.

Following this general pattern of interconnectivity, we can clearly construct a network with any desired number of input units, hidden units, and output units, depending on the size of the vectors that need processing. And we can begin to see the point of having a two-tiered arrangement if we consider what such a network can do when confronted with a real problem. The crucial point to remember is that we can *modify* the synaptic weights in the overall system, so as to implement whatever vector-to-vector transformation we want.

Perceptual Recognition: Learning By Example   Our sample problem is as follows. We are the command crew of a submarine, whose mission will take it into the shallow waters of an enemy harbor, a harbor whose bottom is sprinkled with explosive mines. We need to avoid these mines, and we can at least detect them with our sonar system, which sends out a pulse of sound and then listens for the returning echo in case the pulse bounces off some solid object lying on the bottom. Unfortunately, a sizeable *rock* also returns a sonar echo, an echo that is indistinguishable to the casual ear from a genuine mine echo (figure 7.18).

This is frustrating, because the target harbor is also well sprinkled with largish rocks. The situation is further complicated by the fact that

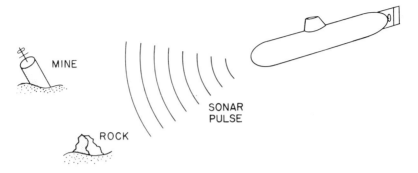

Figure 7.18

mines come in various shapes and lie in various orientations relative to the arriving sonar pulse. And so do rocks. So the echoes returning from each type of object also display considerable variation within each class. On the face of it, the situation looks hopelessly confused.

How might we prepare ourselves to distinguish the explosive mine echoes from the benign rock echoes, so that we may undertake our mission in confidence? As follows. We first assemble, on recording tape, a large set of sonar echoes from what we know to be genuine mines of various types and in various positions. These are mines that we have deliberately laid out, for test purposes, on the bottom of our own coastal waters. We do the same for rocks of various kinds, and of course we keep careful track of which echoes are which. We end up with, say, fifty samples of each.

We then put each echo through a simple spectral analyzer, which yields up information of the sort displayed in the leftmost part of figure 7.19. This just shows how much sound energy the given echo contains at each of the various sound frequencies that make it up. It is a way of quantifying the overall character of any given echo. By itself, this analysis doesn't help us much, since the collected diagrams still don't seem to display any obvious uniformities or regular differences among the echoes. But now let us bring a neural network into the picture. (See again figure 7.19, the rightmost part. This is a simplified version of a network explored by Gorman and Sejnowski. Note that it has been turned on its side, relative to figure 7.17.)

This network is organized on the same lines as the simple network of figure 7.17, but it has 13 input units, 7 hidden units, 2 output units, and a total of 105 synaptic connections. The activity levels of each unit, we shall assume, vary between zero and one. Remember also that the synaptic weights of the system can be adjusted to whatever values are

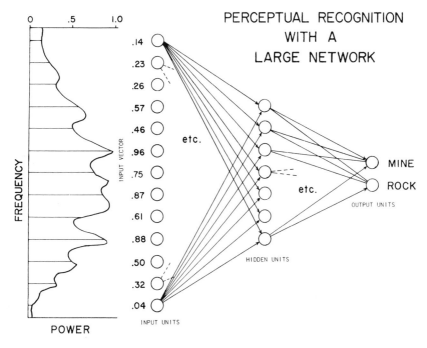

Figure 7.19

needed. But we do not know what values are needed. So at the beginning of the experiment, the connections are given randomly distributed weights. The transformation that the network performs is thus unlikely to be of any use to us. But we proceed as follows.

We take a mine echo from our store of samples, and we use the frequency analyzer to sample its energy levels at 13 different frequencies. This gives us the input vector, which has 13 elements. We then enter this vector into the network by stimulating each of the 13 input units by an appropriate amount, as indicated in figure 7.19. This vector is propagated swiftly forward through the two-stage network, and it produces a two-element output vector in the output units. What we would *like* the network to produce is the vector ⟨1, 0⟩, which is our conventional output vector coding for a *mine*. But given the random weights, that correct output would be a miracle. Most likely it produces some accidental and wholly boring vector like ⟨.49, .51⟩, which tells us next to nothing.

But we are not discouraged. We calculate, by simple subtraction, the difference between the vector we got and the vector we wanted. And we use a special mathematical rule, called the *generalized delta rule*, to calculate small changes for the weights of the system. The idea is to modify those weights that were most responsible for the network's erroneous output. The weights are then adjusted accordingly.

We then give the system another sample echo—perhaps of a rock this time—and hope for an output vector of $\langle 0, 1 \rangle$, which is our conventional output vector coding for a rock. Most likely, the actual output vector is again a disappointment, a $\langle .47, .53 \rangle$ perhaps. Again we calculate the amount of the error and reapply our special rule for adjusting the weights. Then we try again with a third sample. And so forth.

We do this thousands, perhaps tens of thousands, of times. Or rather, we program a conventional computer, whose memory contains our recorded samples, to serve as the teacher and do all the work for us. This is called *training up the network*. Somewhat surprisingly, the result is that the set of weights gradually relaxes into a final configuration where the system gives a $\langle 1, 0 \rangle$ output vector (or close to it) when and only when the input vector is of a mine; and it gives a $\langle 0, 1 \rangle$ output vector (or close to it) when and only when the input vector is of a rock.

The first remarkable fact in all of this is that there *is* a configuration of synaptic weights that allows the system to distinguish fairly reliably between mine echoes and rock echoes. Such a configuration exists because it turns out that there is after all a rough internal pattern or abstract organization that is characteristic of mine echoes as opposed to rock echoes. And the trained network has managed to lock onto that rough pattern.

If, after training up the network, we examine the activity vectors of the *hidden* units for each of the two kinds of stimulation, we find that such vectors form two entirely disjoint classes. Consider, if you will, an abstract 'vector coding space', a space with 7 axes, one each for the activity levels of each hidden unit. (Think of this space along the lines of the abstract sensory coding spaces in Figure 7.13 and 7.14. The only difference is that this space represents the activity levels of cells farther along in the processing hierarchy.) Any 'mine-like' vector occurring across the hidden units falls into a large subvolume of the space of possible hidden-unit vectors. And any 'rock-like' vector falls into a large but quite *distinct* (nonoverlapping) subvolume of that abstract space.

What the hidden units are doing in a trained network is successfully to code some fairly abstract structural features of mine echoes, features they all have, or all approximate, despite their superficial diversity. And it does the same for rock echoes. It does all this by finding a set of weights that produces disjoint classes of coding vectors for each.

Given success of this sort at the level of the hidden units, what the right-hand half of the trained network does is just transform any hidden-unit mine-like vector into something close to a $\langle 1, 0 \rangle$ vector at the output level, and any hidden-unit rock-like vector into something close to a $\langle 0, 1 \rangle$ vector at the output level. In short, it learns to distinguish between the two subvolumes of the hidden-unit vector space. Vectors close to the center of either volume—these are the 'prototypical' examples of each type of vector—produce a clear verdict at the output level. Vectors close to the boundary dividing the two volumes produce a much less decisive response: a $\langle .4, .6 \rangle$ perhaps. The network's 'guess' at a rock is thus not very confident. But it may be fairly reliable even so.

A lovely by-product of this procedure is the following. If the network is now presented with entirely *new* samples of rock echoes and mine echoes—samples it has never heard before—its output vectors will categorize them correctly straight off, and with an accuracy that is only negligibly lower than the accuracy now shown on the 100 samples on which it was originally trained. The new samples, novel though they are, also produce vectors at the level of the hidden units that fall into one of the two distinguishable subspaces. In short, the 'knowledge' that the system has acquired generalizes reliably to new cases. Our system is finally ready to probe the enemy harbor. We just feed it the threatening sonar returns, and its output vectors will tell us whether or not we are approaching a mine.

What is interesting here is not the proposed military application of the device described; I have used that context solely for dramatic effect. Existing naval technologies can already pick out a beer can on a sandy bottom, and even guess at the brand name, by using quite different principles of analysis. What is interesting, rather is that such a *simple* system can perform the sophisticated recognitional task described above.

That a suitably adjusted network will do this job at all is the first marvel. The second marvel is that there exists a rule that will successfully *shape* the network into the necessary configuration of weights, even if it starts out in a random configuration. That rule makes the system learn from the 100 samples we provide it, plus the errors it produces. This process is called *automated learning by the back-propagation of error*, and it is relentlessly efficient. For it will often find order and structure, all by itself, where initially we see only chaos and confusion. This learning process is an instance of *gradient descent*, because the configuration of weights can be seen as sliding down a variable slope of ever-decreasing errors until it enters the narrow region of a lowest valley, at which the error messages get closer and closer to zero. (See figure 7.20 for a partial representation of this process.) With such small

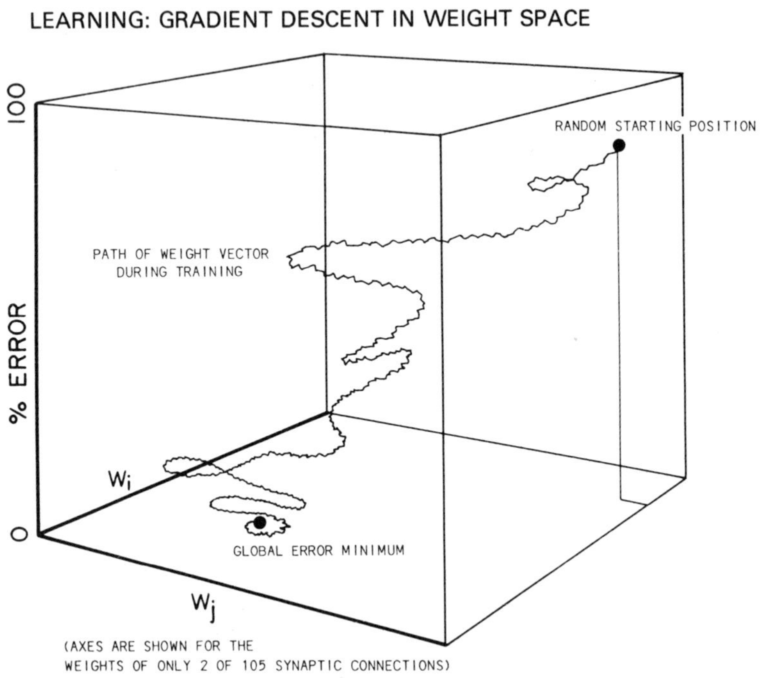

LEARNING: GRADIENT DESCENT IN WEIGHT SPACE

Figure 7.20

errors, the efficiency of further learning naturally goes down, but at that point the system has already reached a high level of reliability.

Training up the network on the many sample echoes may take a couple of hours, but once the system is trained, it will yield up a verdict on any sample in an instant. Being a parallel system, the network transforms the many elements of the input vector all at the same time. Here at last we have the 'perceptual' recognition of complex features on a time scale equal to, or better than, that of living creatures.

Further Examples and
General Observations
I have focused closely on the rock/ mine network in order to provide some real detail on how a parallel network does its job. But the example is only one of many. If mine echoes can be recognized and distinguished from other sounds, then a suitably trained network of this general kind should be able to recognize the various *phonemes* that make up English speech and not be troubled at all by wide differences in the character of people's voices, as traditional AI programs are. Truly effective machine speech-recognition is thus now within reach.

Nor is there anything essentially auditory about the talents of these networks. They can be 'trained up' to recognize complex visual features just as well. A recent network can tell us the 3-D shape and orientation of smoothly curved physical surfaces given only a gray-scale picture of the surface in question. That is, it solves the 'shape-from shading' problem. And once trained, such a network gives its output verdict on any new sample almost instantaneously.

Nor is there anything essentially perceptual about their talents. They can be used to produce interesting motor output just as easily. A rather large network has already learned to solve, for example, the problem of transforming printed text into audible speech (Sejnowski's and Rosenberg's NETtalk). The system uses a vector-coding scheme for input letters, another vector-coding scheme for output phonemes, and it learns the appropriate vector-to-vector transformation. In plain English, it learns to pronounce printed words. And it does so without being given *any* rules to follow whatsoever. This is no mean feat, especially given the irregularities of standard English spelling. The system must learn not just to transform the letter "a" into a certain sound. It must learn to transform "a" into one sound when it occurs in "save", into another sound when it occurs in "have", and into a third when it occurs in "ball". It must learn that "c" is soft in "city", but hard in "cat". And so on and so on.

Initially of course, it does none of this. When fed printed text, its output vector produces, through its sound synthesizer, nonsense babbling rather like a baby's: "nananoonoo noonanana". But each of its erroneous output vectors is analyzed by the standard computer that is monitoring the process. The network's weights are adjusted according to the generalized delta rule. And the quality of its babbling slowly improves. After only ten hours of training on a sample of 1000 words, it produces coherent, intelligible speech given arbitrary English text. And it does so without explicit rules being represented anywhere within the system.

Are there any limits to the transformations that a parallel network of this general kind can perform? Current opinion among workers in the field leans toward the idea that there are no theoretical limits, since the new networks have important features that the networks of the late 50s did not have. Most important, the axonal output signal produced by any unit is not a straight or 'linear' function of the level of excitement in the unit itself. Rather, it follows a kind of S-curve. This simple wrinkle allows a network to compute what are called nonlinear transformations, and this broadens dramatically the range of problems it can handle.

Equally important, the new networks have one or more layers of 'hidden' units intervening between the input and output levels, where the early networks had only an input and an output layer. The advantage of the intervening layer is that, within that layer, the system can explore possible features that are not explicitly represented in the input vectors. It can thus stumble onto regularities that lie behind or underneath the superficial regularities that connect the features that are explicit in the input vectors. This allows the system to *theorize*. To take an example close at hand, what the hidden units in the mine/rock network really learn to code, it turns out, is whether the sonar pulse has bounced off something made of *metal* or *nonmetal*.

Third, current networks can be shaped by the back-propagation algorithm: the generalized delta rule. This recent discovery is a very powerful learning rule, for it allows a network to explore the vector space of its hidden units and to find effective transformations of all possible kinds, both linear and nonlinear. It allows a large network to *find* a complex set of weights that we could never have identified as appropriate beforehand. This is a major breakthrough in the technology of 'machine learning'.

You can now appreciate why artifical networks have captured so much attention. Their microstructure is similar in many respects to that of the brain, and they have at least some of the same hard-to-simulate functional properties.

How far does the analogy go? Is this really how the brain might work? Let me close this section by addressing a serious problem. With artifical networks, we can build in appropriate systems for calculating output error and for modifying the weights accordingly. (For simplicity's sake, none of our diagrams attempt to show these.) But by what pathways, in a *real* brain, is the output error propagated back to the relevant set of synaptic connections, so their weights can be modified and learning can take place? This question is itself a measure of how valuable it is to have some fresh new theory around, because without that theory we would not even be asking so specific a question, nor peering into specific parts of the brain in hopes of an answer.

When we do look into the cerebellum, for example, we find that it does contain a second major input system: the climbing fibers. To avoid clutter, these were not shown in figure 7.16, but they are easily visualized. A climbing fiber, as its name suggests, is like a thin vine that climbs up the large Purkinje cell from the bottom and wraps itself all around the cell body and around the branches of its bushy dendritic tree. Every Purkinje cell ends up wreathed in climbing fiber, like an oak tree overgrown with ivy. The climbing fibers are thus properly positioned to do exactly the job that is needed, namely, to modify the weights of the many synaptic connections between the parallel fibers and the Purkinje cells.

Unfortunately, we do not yet understand how they might be doing this. Nor are we really sure that they do anything remotely like this. Perhaps cognitive theory will here prompt neuroscience to discover something about the activities of climbing fibers that it did not already know. On the other hand, neuroscientific data may show that an appealing theory of learning in the cerebellum (back-propagation of errors) cannot possibly be right.

This would be only a fleeting disappointment for cognitive theory. There are other learning procedures, of comparable efficiency, that exploit wholly local constraints and do not require any back-propagation. Perhaps the brain uses one of them. Clearly more research needs to be done here. What is encouraging about the situation, beyond the startling successes already recorded, is that AI, Cognitive Science, and Neuroscience are now interacting vigorously. They are now teaching each other, a process from which everyone will profit.

A final observation. According to the style of theory we have here been exploring, it is activity vectors that form the most important kind of representation within the brain. And it is vector-to-vector transformations that form the most important kind of computation. This may or may not be correct, but it does give some real substance to the earlier suggestion of the eliminative materialist (section 2.5) that the concepts of folk psychology need not capture the dynamically significant states and activities of the mind. The elements of cognition, as sketched in the preceding pages, have a character unfamiliar to common sense. Perhaps we should actively expect that, as our theoretical understanding here increases, our very conception of the phenomena we are trying to explain will undergo significant revision as well. This is a common pattern throughout the history of science, and there is no reason why Cognitive Science should prove any exception.

Suggested Readings

Rumelhart, D. E., Hinton, G. E., and Williams, R. J., "Learning Representations by Back-propagating Errors," *Nature*, 323, (9 Oct., 1986): pp. 533–36.

Sejnowski, T. J., and Rosenberg, C. R., "Parallel Networks that Learn to Pronounce English Text," *Complex Systems*, vol. 1 (1987).

Churchland, P. S., and Sejnowski, T. J., "Neural Representation and Neural Computation,' *Neural Connections and Mental Computation*, ed. Nadel, L. (Cambridge, MA: The MIT Press, 1988).

Rumelhart, D. E., and McClelland, J. L., *Parallel Distributed Processing: Explorations in the Microstructure of Cognition* (Cambridge, MA: The MIT Press, 1986).

Chapter 8
Expanding Our Perspective

---

1. The Distribution of Intelligence in the Universe

The weight of evidence, as surveyed in the preceding chapters, indicates that conscious intelligence is a wholly natural phenomenon. According to a broad and growing consensus among philosophers and scientists, conscious intelligence is the activity of suitably organized matter, and the sophisticated organization responsible for it is, on this planet at least, the outcome of billions of years of chemical, biological, and neurophysiological evolution.

If intelligence develops naturally, as the universe unfolds, then might it not have developed, or be developing, at many places throughout the universe? The answer is clearly yes, unless the planet Earth is utterly unique in possessing the required physical constitution, or the required energetic circumstances. Is it unique in the relevant respects? Let us examine the evolutionary process, as we now understand it, and see what the process requires.

Energy Flow and the Evolution of Order
Basically, it requires a system of physical elements (such as atoms) capable of many different combinations, and a flow of energy (such as sunlight) through the system of elements. This describes the situation on the prebiological earth, some 4 billion years ago, during the period of purely chemical evolution. The flow or flux of energy, into the system and then out again, is absolutely crucial. In a system *closed* to the entry and exit of external energy, the energy-rich combinations will gradually break up and distribute their energy among the energy-poor elements until the level of energy is everywhere the same throughout the system—this is the *equilibrium* state. Like water, one might say, energy seeks its own level; it tends to flow 'downhill' until the level is everywhere the same.

This humble analogy expresses the essential content of a fundamental physical law called the Second Law of Thermodynamics: In a closed system not already in equilibrium, any energy exchanges tend ruthlessly to move the system toward equilibrium. And once a system has reached this lowest or equilibrium state, it tends to remain there forever—a uniform, undifferentiated murk. The formation of complex, interesting, and energy-rich structures is then profoundly unlikely, since that would require that some of the system's internal energy flow back 'uphill' again. It would require that a significant energy *im*balance spontaneously appear within the system. And this is what the Second Law effectively prohibits. Evidently, the evolution of complex structures is not to be found in a closed system.

If a system is open to a continuous flux of energy, however, then the situation is completely transformed. For a schematic illustration, consider a glass box, full of water, with a constant heat source at one end, and a constant heat sink (something to absorb heat energy) at the other, as in figure 8.1. Dissolved in the water is some nitrogen and some carbon dioxide. One end of the box will grow quite hot, but as fast as the fire pours energy into this end of the system, it is conducted away toward the cooler end and out again. The average temperature inside the box is therefore a constant.

Consider the effect this will have on the thin soup inside the box. At the hot end of the box, the high-energy end, the molecules and atoms absorb this extra energy and are raised to excited states. As they drift around the system, these energized parts are free to form high-energy chemical bonds with each other, bonds that would have been statistically impossible with the system in global equilibrium. A variety of complex chemical compounds is therefore likely to form and to collect toward the cool end of the system, compounds of greater variety and greater complexity than could have been formed without the continuous flux of heat energy. Collectively, carbon, hydrogen, oxygen, and nitrogen are capable of literally millions of different chemical com-

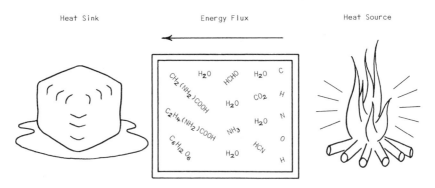

Figure 8.1

binations. With the heat flux turned on, this partially open or *semiclosed* system starts vigorously to explore these combinatorial possibilities.

It is easy to see that a kind of competition is then taking place inside the box. Some types of molecule are not very stable, and will tend to fall apart soon after formation. Other types will be made of sterner stuff, and will tend to hang around for awhile. Other types, though very unstable, may be formed very frequently, and so there will be quite a few of them in the system at any given time. Some types catalyze the formation of their own building blocks, thus enhancing further formation. Other types engage in mutually beneficial catalytic cycles, and form a symbiotic pair of prosperous types. In these ways, and others, the various types of molecules *compete* for dominance of the liquid environment. Those types with high stability and/or high formation rates will form the largest populations.

The typical result of such a process is that the system soon displays a great many instances of a fairly small variety of distinct types of complex, energy-storing molecules. (Which types, from the millions of types possible, actually come to dominate the system is dependent on and highly sensitive to the initial makeup of the soup, and to the flux level.) The system displays an order, and a complexity, and an un-balanced energy distribution that would be unthinkable without the flux of energy through the system. The flux pumps the system. It forces the system away from its initial chaos, and toward the many forms of order and complexity of which it is capable. What was improbable has become inevitable.

The preceding experiment is schematic, concocted to illustrate a general principle, but instances of it have actually been performed. In a now famous experiment, Urey and Miller, in 1953, recreated the earth's prebiotic atmosphere (hydrogen, methane, ammonia, and water) and subjected a flaskful of it to a steady electrical discharge. After several days of this energy flux, examination of the flask's contents showed that many complex organic compounds had formed, including a number of different amino acids, the units from which protein molecules are constructed. Other versions of the experiment tried different energy sources (ultraviolet light, heat, shock waves), and all displayed the same pattern: an energy flux induces order and complexification within a semiclosed system.

Nature has also performed this experiment—with the entire earth, and with billions of other planets. For the earth as a whole is also a semiclosed system, with the sun as the energy source, and the black void surrounding us as the low-temperature energy sink (figure 8.2). Solar energy has been flowing through this gigantic system for well over four thousand million years, patiently exploring the endless possibilities for order, structure, and complexity inherent in the matter it contains. Small wonder it has outperformed the artificial systems described.

From this perspective it is apparent that *any* planet will support a rich evolutionary process, if it possesses a rich variety of elements in some liquid solution, and enjoys a suitable energy flux from a nearby star. Roughly how many planets, in our own Milky Way galaxy, meet these conditions?

The Distribution of Evolutionary Sites   There are roughly 100 billion, or 10^{11}, stars in our galaxy. How many of them possess planets? Theories of stellar formation, spectrographic studies of stellar rotation, and telescopic studies of the dynamic effects of dark companions agree in indicating that effectively all stars except the superhot giants possess a planetary system of some kind. The superhot giants are but a small percentage of the stellar population, so their deletion still leaves us close to 10^{11} planetary systems in the galaxy.

How many of these will contain a planet suitably constituted and suitably placed? Suitable constitution suggests that we should consider only second-generation systems, formed from the debris of earlier stellar explosions, since these are the main source of the elements beyond hydrogen and helium. This leaves us rather less than half of the available systems, so we are down to about 10^{10}. In these remaining systems, planets with an acceptable constitution promise to be fairly common. In our system alone, Earth, Mars, and two of Jupiter's moons show

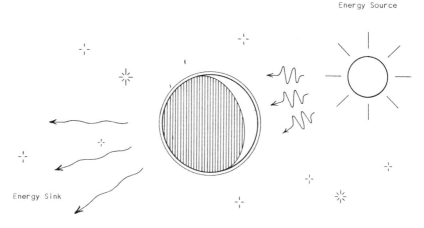

Figure 8.2

significant water, if we demand water as our evolutionary solvent. Jupiter's moons have an extra significance, since giant Jupiter and its twelve-plus satellites almost constitute a miniature solar system in their own right, the only other example available for close study. Interestingly, Jupiter's second and third satellites, Europa and Ganymede, each contain about as much water as the entire Earth: though smaller in area, their oceans are very much deeper than ours. If we may generalize from these two systems then, water planets will be found across a wide range of stellar systems, and some systems will boast two or more.

Nor do water planets exhaust the possibilities. Liquid ammonia and liquid methane are common solvents also, and they are entirely capable of sustaining evolutionary processes. Such oceans occur on much colder planets, and would sustain the exploration of chemical bonds of much lower energy than characterize the biochemistry of Earth. Those bracing environments constitute an alternative evolutionary niche. Altogether, suitable constitution seems not to be a problem. Let us stick with an estimate of at least 10^{10} planets as suitably constituted for significant chemical evolution.

How many of these will be suitably placed, relative to the energy-supplying star? A planet's orbit must be within its star's 'life zone'— far enough from the star to avoid boiling its solvent away, and yet close enough to keep it from freezing solid. For water that zone is fairly wide, and there is a better than even chance that some planetary orbit will fall inside it. We need a *water* planet inside it, however, and these are perhaps only one in every ten planets. Let us estimate, conservatively, that only one in a hundred of our remaining systems contains a suitably placed water planet. Suitably placed ammonia and methane planets are also to be expected, but the same considerations yield a similar estimate for them, and we are left with an estimate of roughly 10^8 planets that are both suitably placed and suitably constituted.

This estimate assumed a star like our sun. But while the sun is already a smallish and undistinguished star, most stars are smaller still, and cooler, and will thus have smaller life zones. This could reduce the chances of suitable placement by another one or two factors of ten. Even so, sun-sized stars make up roughly 10 percent of the relevant population, and their consideration alone would leave us with at least 10^7 blue-ribbon planets.

Our conservative estimate, therefore, is that the evolutionary process is chugging briskly away, at some stage or other, on at least 10,000,000 planets within this galaxy alone.

Life and Intelligence   What is significant about this number is that it is large. The kind of process that produced us is apparently common throughout the universe. The conclusion is exciting, but the real question here remains unanswered: In how many of these cases has the evolutionary process articulated matter to the level of actual *life*, and in how many of these has it produced *conscious intelligence*?

These fractions are impossible to estimate with any confidence, since that would require an understanding of the *rates* at which evolutionary development takes place, and of the alternative paths it can pursue. So far, we have an insufficient grasp of evolution's volatile dynamics to unravel these matters. We are reduced to exploring relevant considerations, but these can still be informative. Let us start with the common conception, hinted at in the preceding paragraph, that evolution has two large and discontinuous gaps to bridge: the gap between nonlife and life, and the gap between unconsciousness and consciousness. Both of these distinctions, so entrenched in common sense, embody a degree of *mis*conception. In fact, neither distinction corresponds to any well-defined or unbridgeable discontinuity in nature.

Consider the notion of life. If we take the capacity for self-replication as its essential feature, then its emergence need represent no discontinuity. Molecules that catalyze the formation of their own building blocks represent a lower position on the same spectrum. One need only imagine a series of progressively more efficient and fast-acting molecules of this kind, and we can culminate smoothly in a molecule that catalyzes its building blocks in sequence so they may hook up as fast as they are produced—a self-replicating molecule. There is no discontinuity here, no gulf to be bridged. The *environment* may display discontinuities, as the efficiency of a certain replicator passes a critical point relative to its competition, but this is a discontinuity in the consequences of self-replication, not in the mechanisms that produce it.

On the other hand, mere self-replication may be too simple a conception of life. There are some grounds for rejecting it. We can imagine some very simple molecules that, in a suitably artificial and contrived chemical environment, would replicate themselves. But this alone need not tempt us to count them as alive. In any case, there is a more penetrating characterization of life at hand, which we can illustrate with the cell, the smallest unit of life, according to some accounts. A cell is itself a tiny semiclosed self-organizing system, within the larger semiclosed system of the earth's biosphere. The energy flowing through a cell serves to maintain, and to increase, the order internal to the cell. In most cells the energy flux is chemical—they ingest energy-rich molecules and pirate the energy they release—but cells capable of photosynthesis make direct use of the solar flux to pump their metabolic processes. All of this suggests that we define a living thing as any semiclosed physical system that exploits the order it already possesses, and the energy flux through it, in such a way as to maintain and/or increase its internal order.

This characterization does capture something deeply important about the things we commonly count as alive. And it embraces comfortably the multicelled organisms, for a plant or animal is also a semiclosed system, composed of tiny semiclosed systems: a vast conspiracy of cells rather than (just) a vast conspiracy of molecules. Even so, the definition has some mildly surprising consequences. If we accept it, a beehive counts as a living thing. So does a termite colony. And so does a human city. In fact, the entire biosphere counts as a living thing. For all of these things meet the definition proposed.

At the other end of the spectrum—and this returns us to the discontinuity issue—some very simple systems can lay claim to life. Consider the glowing teardrop of a candle flame: this too is a semiclosed system, and though its internal order is small and its self-maintenance feeble, it may just barely meet the conditions of the definition proposed. Other borderline systems will present similar problems. Should we reject the definition then? No. The wiser lesson is that living systems are distinguished from nonliving systems only by degrees. There is no metaphysical gap to be bridged: only a smooth slope to be scaled, a slope measured in degrees of order and in degrees of self-regulation.

The same lesson emerges when we consider conscious intelligence. We have already seen how consciousness and intelligence come in different grades, spread over a broad spectrum. Certainly intelligence is not unique to humans: millions of other species display it in some degree. If we define intelligence, crudely, as the possession of a complex set of appropriate responses to the changing environment, then even the humble potato displays a certain low cunning. No metaphysical discontinuities emerge here.

But that definition is too crude. It leaves out the developmental or creative aspect of intelligence. Consider then the following, more penetrating, definition. A system has intelligence just in case it exploits the *information* it already contains, and the energy flux through it (this includes the energy flux through its sense organs), in such a way as to *increase* the information it contains. Such a system can *learn*, and that seems to be the central element of intelligence.

This improved characterization does capture something deeply important about the things we commonly count as intelligent. And I hope the reader is already struck by the close parallels between this definition of intelligence, and our earlier definition of life as the exploitation of contained order, and energy flux, to get more order. These parallels are important for the following reason. If the possession of information can be understood as the possession of some internal physical order that bears some systematic relation to the environment, then the operations of intelligence, abstractly conceived, turn out to be just a high-grade version of the operations characteristic of life, save that they are even more intricately coupled to the environment.

This hypothesis is consistent with the brain's use of energy. The production of large amounts of specific kinds of order requires a very substantial energy flux. And while the brain constitutes only 2 percent of the body's mass, it consumes, when highly active, over 20 percent of the resting body's energy budget. The brain too is a semiclosed system, a curiously high-intensity one, whose ever changing microscopic order reflects the world in impressive detail. Here again, intelligence represents no discontinuity. Intelligent life is just life, with a high thermodynamic intensity and an especially close coupling between internal order and external circumstance.

What all this means is that, given energy enough, and time, the phenomena of both life *and* intelligence are to be expected as among the natural products of planetary evolution. Energy enough, and planets, there are. Has there been time? On Earth, there has been time enough, but what of the other 10^7 candidates? Our uncertainty here is very great. A priori, the probability is vanishingly *small* that we are the very first planet to develop intelligent life: no better than one chance in 10^7. And the probability shrinks further when we consider that stars had already been pumping planets with energy for at least 10 billion years when the Sun/Earth system first condensed into being, some 4.5 billion years ago. If anything, we entered the evolutionary race with a long handicap. On the other hand, evolutionary rates may be highly volatile, varying by orders of magnitude as a function of subtle planetary variables. That would render our time handicap insignificant, and we might yet be the first planet in our galaxy to develop intelligence.

No decision made here can command confidence, but a forced decision, made under the preceding uncertain assumptions, would have to guess that something on the order of half of the relevant candidates are behind us, and half are ahead. This 'best guess' entails that something like 10^6 planets in this galaxy alone have *already* produced highly intelligent life.

Does this mean that we should expect little green men in flying saucers to frequent our atmosphere? It does not. Not even if we accept the 'best guess'. The reasons are important, and there are three of them. The first reason is the spatial scattering of the 10^6 planets. Our galaxy has a volume of over 10^{14} cubic light-years (that is, the distance covered in a year's time when moving at the speed of light = 186,000 miles per second × 1 year, which is nearly 6 trillion miles), and 10^6 planets scattered throughout this volume will have an average distance between them of over 500 light-years. That is a most inconvenient distance for casual visits.

The second and perhaps more important reason is temporal scatter. We cannot assume that all of these 10^6 planets will develop intelligent life simultaneously. Nor can we be certain that, once developed, intelligent life lasts for very long. Accidents happen, degeneration sets in, self-destruction occurs. Suppose, for illustration, that the average lifetime of intelligence on any planet is 100 million years (this is the interval between the appearance of the early mammals and the nuclear holocaust that might destroy us within the century). If these intelligent stretches are scattered uniformly in time, then any planet with intelligence is likely to have only 10^4 concurrently intelligent planets for company, with an average distance between them of 2,500 light-years. Moreover, nothing guarantees that those other cradles of intelligence concurrently boast anything more intelligent than field mice, or sheep. Our own planet has surpassed that level only recently. And highly intelligent, high-technology civilizations may last on average only 1,000 years, by reason of some inherent instabilities. In that case they will almost always be utterly and tragically alone in the galaxy. The case for highly intelligent company is starting to look rather thin.

And so it is, if we assign suicidal tendencies to all potential company. If we do not, then we may return to a more optimistic estimate of current company. If we assume an average duration for intelligent life of between 1 and 5 billion years, then temporal scatter will still leave us with 10^5 planets concurrently abreast or ahead of us in evolutionary development. This may seem finally to hold promise for some little green men and some edifying communication, if only by radio telescope. But it does not, for the third and most important reason of all: the potentially endless variation in the different *forms* that life and intelligence can take.

Our biosphere has been articulated into individual units of independent life: cells and multicelled organisms. None of this is strictly necessary. Some biospheres may have evolved into a single, unified, massively complex and highly intelligent 'cell' that girdles the entire planet. Others may have synthesized their cells, or multicelled elements, into a similarly unified singular planetary individual. For one of us to try to communicate with such an entity might be like a single bacterial cell in the local swamp attempting to communicate with a human, by emitting a few chemicals. The larger entity is simply not 'interested'.

Even with more familiar creatures, a different environment can demand different sense organs, and different sense organs can mean very different brains (generally speaking, brains must evolve from the sensory periphery inward, developing in ways that serve the modalities available). Creatures that navigate by felt electric fields, hunt by direction finders in the far infrared, guide close manipulation by stereoaudition in the 50-kilohertz range, and communicate by fugues of aromatic hydrocarbons are unlikely to think in the same grooves as a human.

Strange sense organs aside, the particular cluster of cognitive talents found in us need not characterize an alien species. For example, it is possible to be highly intelligent and yet lack all capacity for manipulating numbers, even the ability to count past five. It is equally possible to be highly intelligent and yet lack any capacity for understanding or manipulating language. Such isolated deficits occasionally occur in humans of otherwise exemplary mental talents. The first is a rare but familiar syndrome called *acalculia*. The second, more common, affliction is called *global aphasia*. We must not expect, therefore, that a highly intelligent alien species must inevitably know the laws of arithmetic, or be able to learn a system like language, or have any inkling that these things even exist. These reflections suggest further that there may be fundamental cognitive abilities of whose existence *we* are totally unaware!

Finally, we must not expect that the goals or concerns of an alien intelligent species will resemble our own, or even be intelligible to us. The consuming aim of an entire species might be to finish composing the indefinitely long magnetic symphony begun by their prehistoric ancestors, a symphony where the young are socialized by learning to sing its earlier movements. A different species might have a singular devotion to the pursuit of higher mathematics, and their activities might make as much sense to us as the activities of a university mathematics department would make to a Neanderthal. Equally important, racial goals themselves undergo evolutionary change, either genetic or cultural. The dominant goals of our own species, 5,000 years hence, may bear no relation to our current concerns. All of which means that we cannot expect an intelligent alien species to share the enthusiasms and concerns that characterize our own fleeting culture.

The point of the preceding discussion has been to put questions about the nature of intelligence into a broader perspective than they usually enjoy, and to emphasize the extremely general or abstract nature of this natural phenomenon. Current human intelligence is but one variation on a highly general theme. Even if, as does seem likely, intelligence *is* fairly widespread within our galaxy, we can infer almost nothing about what those other intelligent species must be doing, or about what form their intelligence takes. If the theoretical definition of intelligence given earlier is correct, then we may infer that they must be using *energy* (perhaps in copious quantities) and creating *order*, and that at least some of the order created has something to do with sustaining fruitful interactions with their environment. Beyond that, everything is possible. For us, as well as for them.

Suggested Readings

Schrödinger, E., *What Is Life?* (Cambridge: Cambridge University Press, 1945).

Shklovskii, I. S., and Sagan, C., *Intelligent Life in the Universe* (New York: Dell, 1966).

Cameron, A. G. W., *Interstellar Communication: The Search for Extraterrestrial Life* (New York: Benjamin, 1963).

Sagan, C., and Drake, F., "Search for Extraterrestrial Intelligence," *Scientific American*, vol. 232 (May 1975).

Morowitz, H., *Energy Flow in Biology* (New York: Academic Press, 1968).

Feinberg, G., and Shapiro, R., *Life beyond Earth* (New York: William Morrow and Company, 1980).

2. The Expansion of Introspective Consciousness

By way of bringing this book to a close, let us return from the universe at large, and refocus our attention on the phenomenon of introspective awareness or self-consciousness. I have been employing a very general and neutral conception of introspection throughout this book, which can be sketched as follows.

We have a large variety of internal states and processes. We also have certain innate mechanisms for discriminating the occurrence of some of these states and processes from their nonoccurrence, and for discriminating them one from another. And when we invoke and attend to that discriminatory activity, we can respond to it with explicitly conceptual moves—that is, with more or less appropriate *judgments* about those internal states and processes, judgments framed in the familiar concepts of common sense: "I have a sensation of pink," "I feel dizzy," "I have a pain," and so forth. We thus have some access, however incomplete, to our own internal activities.

Self-knowledge is supposed to be a good thing according to almost everyone's ideology. How then might we improve or enhance this introspective access? Surgical or genetic modification of our innate introspective mechanisms is one possibility, but not a realistic one in the short term. Short of this, perhaps we can learn to make more refined and penetrating use of the discriminatory mechanisms we already possess.

The modalities of external sense provide many precedents for this suggestion. Consider the enormous increase in discriminatory skill (and theoretical insight) that spans the gap between an untrained child's auditory apprehension of Beethoven's Fifth Symphony, and the same person's auditory apprehension of the same symphony forty years later, heard in his capacity as conductor of the orchestra performing it. What was before a single voice is now a mosaic of distinguishable elements. What was before a dimly apprehended tune is now a rationally structured sequence of distinguishable chords supporting an appropriately related melody line. The conductor hears far more than the child did, and probably far more than most of us do.

Other modalities provide similar examples. Consider the chemically sophisticated wine taster, for whom the gross "red wine" category used by most of us divides into a network of fifteen or twenty distinguishable elements: ethanol, glycol, fructose, sucrose, tannin, acid, carbon dioxide, and so forth, whose relative concentrations he can estimate accurately. He tastes far more than we do. Or consider the astronomer, for whom the speckled black dome of her youth has become a visible abyss, distributing nearby planets, yellow dwarf stars, blue and red giants, and even a remote galaxy or two, all discriminable as such and locatable in three-dimensional space with her unaided (*unaided*) eye. She sees far more than we do. Just how much more is difficult to appreciate in advance of actually acquiring the relevant skills.

In each of these cases, what is finally mastered is a conceptual framework—whether musical, chemical, or astronomical—a framework that embodies far more wisdom about the relevant sensory domain than is *immediately* apparent to untutored discrimination. Such frameworks are usually a cultural heritage, pieced together over many generations, and their mastery supplies a richness and penetration to our sensory lives that would be impossible in their absence.

Turning now to introspection, it is evident that our introspective lives are already the extensive beneficiaries of this phenomenon. The introspective discriminations we make are for the most part learned; they are acquired with practice and experience, often quite slowly. And the specific discriminations we learn to make are those it is useful for us to make. Generally, those are the discriminations that others are already making, the discriminations embodied in the psychological vocabulary of the language we learn. The conceptual framework for psychological states that is embedded in ordinary language is, as we saw in chapters 3 and 4, a modestly sophisticated theoretical achievement in its own right, and it shapes our matured introspection profoundly. If it embodied substantially *less* wisdom in its categories and connecting generalizations, our introspective apprehension of our internal states and activities would be much diminished, though our native discriminatory mechanisms remained the same. Correlatively, if it embodied substantially *more* wisdom about our inner nature than it currently does, our introspective discrimination and recognition could be very much *greater* than it is, though our native discriminatory mechanisms remained the same.

This brings me to the final positive suggestion of this chapter. If materialism, in the end, is true, then it is the conceptual framework of a completed neuroscience that will embody the essential wisdom about our inner nature. (I here ignore, for now, the subtleties that divide the various forms of materialism.) Consider then the possibility of learning to describe, conceive, and introspectively apprehend the teeming intricacies of one's inner life within the conceptual framework of a 'completed' neuroscience, or one advanced far beyond its current state. Suppose we trained our native mechanisms to make a new and more detailed set of discriminations, a set that corresponded not to the primitive psychological taxonomy of ordinary language, but to some more penetrating taxonomy of states drawn from a 'completed' neuroscience. And suppose we trained ourselves to respond to that reconfigured activity with judgments that were framed, as a matter of habit, in the appropriate concepts from neuroscience.

If the examples of the symphony conductor, the wine expert, and the astronomer provide a fair parallel, then the enhancement in our introspective vision could approximate a revelation. Glucose consumption in the forebrain, dopamine levels in the thalamus, the coding vectors in specific neural pathways, resonances in the nth layer of the peristriatal cortex, and countless other neurophysiological and neurofunctional niceties could be moved into the objective focus of our introspective discrimination and conceptual recognition, just as Gmin7 chords and A+9 chords are moved into the objective focus of a trained musician's auditory discrimination and conceptual recognition. We shall of course have to *learn* the conceptual framework of the projected neuroscience in order to pull this off. And we shall have to practice to gain skill in applying those concepts in our noninferential judgments. But that seems a small price to pay, given the projected return.

This suggestion was initially floated in our discussion of eliminative materialism, but the possibility is equally open to the other materialist positions. If the reductive materialist is right, then the taxonomy of folk psychology will map more or less smoothly onto some substructure of the taxonomy of a 'completed' neuroscience. But that new taxonomy will still embody by far the more penetrating insight into our nature. And if the functionalist is right, then the 'completed' theory will be more abstract and computational in its vision of our internal activities. But that vision will still surpass the simple kinematic and explanatory conceptions of common sense. In all three cases, the move to the new framework promises a comparable advance, both in general knowledge and in self-understanding.

I suggest then, that the genuine arrival of a materialist kinematics and dynamics for psychological states and cognitive processes will constitute not a gloom in which our inner life is eclipsed or suppressed, but rather a dawning, in which its marvelous intricacies are finally revealed—even, if we apply ourselves, in self-conscious introspection.

Index